The Art of **Significance**

The Art of **Significance**

ACHIEVING THE LEVEL

BEYOND SUCCESS

DAN CLARK

PORTFOLIO / PENGUIN

PORTFOLIO / PENGUIN
Published by the Penguin Group
Penguin Group (USA) Inc., 375 Hudson Street,
New York, New York 10014, USA

USA / Canada / UK / Ireland / Australia / New Zealand / South Africa / China

Penguin Books Ltd, Registered Offices: 80 Strand, London WC2R 0RL, England
For more information about the Penguin Group visit penguin.com

First published in 2013 by Portfolio / Penguin,
a member of Penguin Group (USA) Inc.

LIBRARY OF CONGRESS CATALOGING IN PUBLICATION DATA

Clark, Dan.
The art of significance : achieving the level beyond success / Dan Clark.
p. cm.
ISBN 978-1-59184-574-4
1. Success.   2. Character.   3. Conduct of life.   I. Title.
BJ1611.2.C487 2012
170'.44—dc23
2012036946

PRINTED IN THE UNITED STATES OF AMERICA
1   3   5   7   9   10   8   6   4   2

Set in ITC Giovanni Std
Designed by Alissa Amell

To anyone
who is crazy enough to believe that
he or she can actually change the world
by
seeing things as they really are,
connecting the head and the heart,
embracing each struggle,
riding out every cycle,
increasing your value,
diversifying your impact,
managing your priorities,
multiplying your connections,
creating opportunities in change,
maximizing your income per hour,
thinking like a self-contained business,
and living an extraordinary life that mattered to
your family, friends, coworkers, community, and country.

Foreword

This book is not a creation, but an observation. Originally, my long-time friend and colleague Dan Clark set out to blaze a new trail to success, but on the way he found something more. Dan realized that our greatest human challenge lies not in choosing our path, but in choosing to be unique and significant among the masses. The result isn't just a book about business leadership and management, but a complete instruction manual for the art of being fully alive. Just as Dan is larger than life and his platform speeches inspire and change lives, this book will also take you to the next level and forever impact who you are, what you do, and why and how you do it.

Dan writes like he speaks, which means this book will challenge your beliefs, making you laugh and cry and think and feel as it suggests how to become more of who you already are. While Dan teaches us the Twelve Highest Universal Laws of Life-Changing Leadership, he also takes us on an emotional roller-coaster ride through the forgotten fundamentals of what it takes to create and run an extremely profitable, high-performance, world-class organization in which everybody wants to work and with whom everyone wants to do business. There is no better person or more qualified expert than Dan to teach us why great is not good enough, what it means to walk on higher ground, and how to live our lives by the highest standards of concept and conduct.

If you subscribe to and obey the laws promulgated in this book, you will most definitely transform yourself and your organization from successful to significant. You will become an extraordinary thought leader, growth leader, and people builder as a corporate executive, military officer, noncommissioned officer (NCO), educator, coach, spouse, parent, and friend. Read on. Pass it along. I promise you will never be the same!

—Jack Canfield,
Co-creator, #1 *New York Times* bestselling series
Chicken Soup For The Soul®;

Coauthor, *The Success Principles*
www.jackcanfield.com

Contents

successful (*adjective*)

1: producing results in competition with others; getting what you think you want relative to what others have.

2: achieving wealth, influence, and popularity through accomplishments that endure only while you are alive.

significant (*adjective*)

1: producing desired results by competing against *yourself;* believing in something larger than life; giving in to a higher purpose; making a difference, not just a living; wanting what you get.

2: achieving wealth, influence, popularity, *and* admiration, loyalty, and respect through accomplishments that endure even beyond the grave.

highest laws (*noun*)

1: statements of fact, deduced from observation, to the effect that a particular natural or scientific phenomenon always occurs if certain conditions are present.

2: universal, eternal, concentrated truths, packaged for application to a wide variety of circumstances; truths that answer the "why" questions of our lives, helping us make decisions even under the most confusing of circumstances.

Introduction: Successful or Significant?

The most significant beings are those artists whose medium is life itself. The ones who express the inexpressible without brush, hammer, clay or guitar. They neither paint nor sculpt. Their medium is being. Whatever their presence touches has increased life. They see and don't have to draw. They are the artists of being fully alive.

—J. STONE

Do you aspire to be successful—or would you rather be significant?

I first learned about significance while fighting my way back from an injury that cut short my American football career and destroyed my path to a successful life as I understood it.

One day in practice, the coaches divided our group of linebackers and defensive ends into two groups and pushed us fifteen yards apart. The coach blew the whistle and another player and I ran into each other full speed. In a brutal head-on collision, my teammate's helmet hit my helmet and neck, and our shoulders slammed into each other. I lay on the ground in shock, a sharp, piercing pain shooting through my body. I had cracked my neck, severed the axillary nerve in my right deltoid, and suffered a grade-two concussion. By nightfall, my neck was stiff, my arm was numb and dangled by my side, and I perspired profusely, shook, and threw up until I cried myself to sleep.

For the next fourteen months, I was paralyzed both physically and emotionally as my successful and promising life came crashing down. As a teenager, I had focused only on sports and other ways to gain fame and glory. I was a Golden Gloves boxing champion; an intermountain alpine ski racing champion; a motocross champion; and an award-winning football, basketball, and baseball player. I was also an actor, appearing in the weekly CBS television series *47 Happiness Way.* After high school, I had an invitation tryout with Major League Baseball's Kansas City Royals as a pitcher and received many scholarship offers to play Division I college sports. At the University of Utah, I was a projected number one draft pick for the NFL. I had known success and now I had nothing.

People thought I had merely hurt my shoulder, but, in fact, my heart was broken, my dreams were shattered, and life as I knew it was impossible. I couldn't concentrate on work or school. My injury left me with a burning, tingling sensation 24/7 on my entire right side. My social life screeched to a halt because nerve-induced shocks shot up through my right arm, and I inadvertently knocked things over. As an athlete, I had enjoyed celebrity treatment everywhere I went. Now that I was hurt, I was a nobody to those who had previously chanted my name, and soon I was a nobody to myself.

Although thirty years have passed since that dream-shattering day, I regard my injury as one of the best things that ever happened to me. No, the best thing was not the accident but what I learned about myself and who I became while working through the setback. I didn't get what I wanted, but when I answered *why* I needed to get better—focusing on purposes instead of shallow goals, on being whole rather than having fame—I ended up wanting what I got, getting closer to what was really in my heart, learning how to serve others, and finding a significant life much more fulfilling than my previous successes.

But getting to that place of peace was a long and difficult process. Henry David Thoreau wrote that men live lives of quiet desperation, and I was experiencing that firsthand. Sixteen doctors told me I would not get any better, and as their responses came in, I spiraled downward. At one point I didn't know if I could go on and actually planned an exit strategy. But through obedience and trust I was able to stretch and persevere. Eighteen months after my injury, I had fought my way back to a 95 percent recovery.

The question I am most frequently asked is: What took so long? My answer: I was asking the wrong questions. I was asking the doctors *how* to get better, but I should have been asking myself *why* I should get better.

Focusing on *how* had been setting me up for failure because each doctor had had a different theory, and the pain felt so excruciating that quitting before fully recovering seemed easy and reasonable. Without sounding too dramatic, when I was injured, confused, and feeling alone in the dark, I discovered that it takes courage to leap into an abyss, whether for the thrill of adventure or to dispense with a situation that no longer works. It's easier to hesitate, holding on to the familiar, clinging to people, positions, and possessions that are no longer sustaining, because we fear the unknown. We seek a renaissance of spirit, a return to understanding that *being* is more important than *having*, and yet we lose our vitality by resisting the very steps that could help us create a dynamic and fulfilling life.

Obviously, you don't need a life-altering experience to put you on the path to success. But every individual living a life of significance has some sort of recovery story that taught him or her the difference between success and significance. I see mine as akin to the process by which silver is cast into art. As a precious metal, the silver is heated up, but because each vat of the molten metal responds differently to the same temperature, the artist has but one technique to know when the liquid stands ready for pouring into a beautiful shape. Only when the artist can see his face reflecting back at him from the silver is it ready to be molded into something more.

Whenever I have felt the "heat" or have been put to a test to see what I am made of, only when I've looked myself square in the eyes, with the proverbial man in the mirror reflecting back at me, have I been ready to mold and shape the man I am into the *something-more man* that I needed to be. (This is very much like a midlife crisis is, when you realize you're not the person you thought you were going to be. Most men have their midlife crisis at forty. I had mine at twenty-two!)

What Is Significance?

So, what is the difference between significance and success?

Success is getting what you want and finding happiness on a superficial level. Success is achieving goals—without having much purpose behind those goals. Success is creating the life you want—but leaving no legacy and making no difference in the grand scheme of things.

What I'm calling *significance* is a higher state of happiness and fulfillment beyond the merely *successful*. Attaining significance means becoming aware of your purpose and working hard to bring that out in the world. Things happen for a reason, but it's our human responsibility to determine what that reason is—what our purpose is. To the extent that we can come to grips with reality and actually want what we worked hard to get, not merely to get what we want, we open ourselves up to significance. Sadly, too many of us—in fact, almost all of us—give up what we want most in order to obtain the empty success we *think* we want at the moment.

Becoming significant isn't about forgoing mundane dreams of success. It's about homing in on that deeper thing that matters to you, pursuing it, bringing benefit to others, and along the way, also achieving success for yourself, albeit perhaps in a different guise than you might originally have imagined it. Which company will achieve more conventional success—the success-oriented one whose employees, when asked what they do for a living, describe the task they perform every day, or the significant one whose employees energetically describe the purpose of the greater enterprise? Where will you find the elements that fuel sustainable business results, such as a greater sense of pride and loyalty, or the desire to increase productivity and profitability?

Significance is the difference between your average physician, who has succeeded academically and graduated from a recognized medical school, and that rare doctor who travels to a developing country and performs cleft lip/cleft palate surgery on children, seeking no money, recognition, or glory. It's the difference between NBA superstars Allen Iverson and Antoine Walker, who reportedly made over $100 million each in their basketball careers yet are now flat broke, and Magic Johnson, who promotes AIDS awareness and builds movie theaters, restaurants, and shopping malls in depressed neighborhoods, creating jobs and pursuing economic development for the disadvantaged and underserved youth.

Better still, it's the difference between the recording-industry pop stars and Hollywood celebrities with no education who think mansions, cars, and jewelry make them somebody, and my friend and colleague Kareem Abdul-Jabbar, the NBA's all-time leading scorer, who won six world championships and a record six regular season MVP Awards yet says his most significant asset is his mind. Since his retirement, Kareem has become a *New York Times* best-selling author, filmmaker, and inspirational speaker. In 2011 the Obama administration appointed him the U.S. Global Cultural Ambassador. Even more significant, four of Kareem's five children have graduated from college, and his son, Amir, speaks three languages and graduated from medical school in 2012.

On a personal note, the difference between success and significance is a motivational speaker who is all about himself—writing, polishing, and presenting a speech that impresses the audience—and one who seeks to bless, not impress, inspiring the audience to become more of who they already are.

Many people are successful but only a few are significant. Which would you rather be?

The Heights of Significance

My lifetime of thinking about significance came to a head in late October 2010 when I had a rare opportunity to experience a "high flight" aboard a U2 reconnaissance spy plane. At the breathtaking classified altitude of over 70,000 feet, and with tears in my eyes that kept fogging my helmet's visor, I saw the curvature of the earth and witnessed the majesty and endless blackness of space, and at about fifteen miles above the earth's surface, I literally gazed into eternity. It suddenly became obvious to me that the earth was a complete system that each of us needed to take better care of and that the atmosphere is thin and fragile.

Another part of the spiritual experience was realizing that for those few hours, my pilot and I were higher than any other humans, with the exception of the few dedicated individuals living aboard the international space station. I came to reflect on the nature of accomplishment and legacy, and it hit me that personal success, what we do for ourselves, dies with us, but that significance, what we do for others and the world, remains and is ever-lasting.

Given the reality of death, what really matters is not how successful we've become, but whether we've made a difference and left our families, friends, coworkers, neighborhoods, and countries in better shape than we first encountered them. Financial and professional success is impressive, but the significance we hold in the eyes of others is *important*.

When you get down to it, "best" and "great" lack meaning; they're just relative terms whose definition depends on what we compare them against. What most of us don't ever do is learn how to think truly uncommon thoughts so we can do truly uncommon things. Beholden to conventional wisdom, we don't put mental frameworks in place that allow us to understand significance and behaviors that produce it. As a result, lasting happiness eludes us, as do true individuality and real influence over others.

The Art of Significance seeks to equip you emotionally and intellectually to take the higher road through life—and to feel more fulfilled in the process. My journey through the realms of business, sports, the military, and family life has resulted in a time-tested gathering of the Twelve Highest Universal Laws of Life-Changing Leadership that can transform lives and organizations from successful to significant. In presenting these laws, I sharply define what makes a person significant as opposed to merely successful, and in doing so reveal new, more meaningful patterns of action.

You won't find many common thoughts here, nor the usual language and illustrations that fill popular leadership or transformation books. Taking on sacred cows—the work-life balance, the values of hope and patience, the sufficiency of faith, the importance of being a team player, the notion that "great" is good enough—I replace them with less-appreciated but more fundamental concepts like Practicing Obedience, Exercising Perseverance, Proactively Stretching, Trusting Predictability, Knowing the Whole Truth, Focusing on Winning, Doing and Being Right, Seeking Harmony, Accepting Others, Striving to Be Needed and Loved, Establishing Covenant Promises, and Learning Forgiveness. As you find your belief system challenged, I promise that you will experience multiple aha moments that will force your mind to acknowledge the progress, elucidate how things really work, and revolutionize the way you lead, manage, teach, mentor, coach, parent, love, and influence others. For the first time in your life, you'll understand how to live more richly so that your purpose is what you say it is and your life will truly matter. You'll find yourself in a position to make a difference, to guide others so that they, too, not only get what they want, but more important, want what they get.

Finding Our Personal "Why"

You may ask: Isn't it enough to get what we want? Why aim for anything more?

Deep inside, we all know success isn't what it's cracked up to be. Empirical evidence of this abounds, if we care to look. Years ago, a *Fortune* magazine article titled "Why Grade 'A' Executives Get an 'F' as Parents" related that children of successful executives were more likely to suffer a range of emotional and health-related problems than children of less successful parents. The article blamed this phenomenon on executives' long hours and personal characteristics of impatience, perfectionism, efficiency, and intolerance for incompetence and irresponsibility. Similarly, if we consider all the "excellent" and "great" companies spotlighted by business best-sellers, we find that many of them eventually fell and didn't live up to the hype. Successful organizations do share certain positive attributes, but they all too often also share the cancerous qualities and convoluted mind-sets of unsuccessful organizations, so eventually they, too, fall by the wayside.

The real problem with the idea of pursuing success is that we may actually get it. Then what? I played American football with a guy who was 6 feet 8, 285 pounds who could bench-press 500 pounds and who ran a 4.6 second 40-yard dash. The NFL's Philadelphia Eagles drafted him in the second round. Two years later, the Eagles traded him to the Oakland Raiders for a huge signing bonus and a multimillion-dollar contract. Two years after that, he walked out of practice and quit, never to play again. Why? He loved being a football player but he hated playing football. He got what he wanted but didn't want what he got. He loved the money, fame, and celebrity perks, but he hated the nomadic lifestyle, the wild temptations on the road, the obligation to play when injured, and the requirement to stay in shape year-round. He was living a successful existence, but because he was misaligned with his inner voice and purpose, his was not a significant life.

Expanding Your Mind

Significance is an unending *intellectual, emotional,* and *spiritual* journey that leads in turn to real action in the world. Success, by contrast, is but a mere destination. It follows that to become significant, we can't just mindlessly master a set of how-to rules or guidelines; that's the "success" mind-set. Rather, we need to go deeper and initiate a comprehensive shift in how we understand and relate with the world. We don't see things as they are; we see things as *we* are. We must stop satisfying our appetites with the status quo of more money, more toys, bigger houses, more benefits from work, more government bailout programs for being greedy. We must focus on *getting our minds right* and aligning them with our hearts, so that we may be the change we seek in the world. We need to change progressively the way we *think* and trust that the how-to will flow from there. (And it does inevitably follow. As we shall see, the how-to is the easy part.)

I have designed this book to help you push against the grain and further your own intellectual and spiritual growth, so that you can eventually change the way you live. I'll challenge you to think (and rethink) for yourself, something that most of us are not always in-clined to do. Yes, we're all hardwired for progress and inherently yearn to ask, seek, find, and knock to open new intellectual and emotional doors. Yet because our time is limited, even the thought and growth leaders among us remain mired in a stagnant state of success—not because they chose it, but because they don't know what they don't know. We also languish in a success mind-set be-cause our peers influence us. When we put a hard-to-catch horse in the same field with an easy-to-catch horse, we usually wind up with two hard-to-catch horses. When we put a sick child in the same room with a healthy one, we usually wind up with two sick children.

Even people who already feel they have accomplished a lot intel-lectually or academically need to push their minds to expand and grow. Unfortunately, many educators fall into a sterile pattern, busy-ing themselves with taking simple tasks and things and making them complicated. My focus in writing this book was to take some-thing complicated and make it simple. Albert Einstein said, "Most of the things that are really worth knowing cannot be taught, they must be learned." Bertrand Russell noted that "men are born igno-rant, not stupid. They are made stupid by education." With all due respect to academics, the most important function of education at any level is to develop the personality and character of the individ-ual, and that's what this book seeks to accomplish.

Living the Laws

To incite a paradigm shift in your thinking, I invite you to put aside the principles that success-oriented people follow and wrap your mind around my Twelve Laws of Significance. These laws, which bring what we think in alignment with what we *do*, are not new, nor do they belong to me. Revealed to me through my experiences, they have been promulgated by the great philosophers and have been present in the world's religious traditions in various forms for thousands of years. The Twelve Laws include all the other Universal Truths found in the laws of attraction, intention, abundance, and cause and effect; they are constantly at work, even if we are not.

As the following chapters reveal, the success principles we are so familiar with turn out to be only preparatory truths underlying the higher-level laws. While successful people follow the principles, significant individuals do the harder work of obeying the more expansive, comprehensive laws. With the Twelve Laws of Significance in hand, you'll gain the higher awareness you need to make leadership automatic and leave a legacy to your company, coworkers, neighbors, children, and grandchildren. You'll understand more deeply what pursuing service over self really means. You'll know to seek the whole truth in your dealings with others, not merely reaffirm what you already believe. You'll learn to cultivate true love in relationships rather than mere selfish romance. You'll grasp the secret of change—bringing it out from the inside rather than reacting to an external stimulus. Finally, you'll come away eager to do the right thing not because you have to, but because *you can*—not because others expect it, but because *you demand it of yourself.*

To help you more easily translate these laws into automatic thoughts and actions, I've arranged them in the sequential order in which they must be learned. Each chapter contrasts a lower elementary law of life that everybody can follow with the corresponding law that only a select few commit to obey. Using a blend of philo-sophical and psychological insights, case studies, historical exam-ples, military stories, personal experiences, humorous observations, and other material, I suggest how following the laws catapults you above the masses—morally, ethically, emotionally, and in terms of your impact on the world.

How many times have we allowed ourselves to be led down the garden path of personal and professional development only to dis-cover that the principles we had been persuaded to adopt were not absolutes, just some researcher's interpretation based on arbitrarily chosen criteria? This book, by contrast, is the ultimate mental meal and definitive behavior bible for highest-level living. It's not "trendy," and it will never need updating. Rather than the latest self-improvement technique, solution, or secret formula, I present un-changing, universal laws that govern our power to transform and improve.

Even if mere success is your goal, these laws are far more impor-tant to learn than a thousand techniques of improvement. Nothing happens by chance; everything occurs in accordance with universal laws. Life can do for us only what it does through us, and only when we abide by the laws that govern it can we harvest the promised fruits of abundance, prosperity, happiness, health, as well as inner tranquility, comfort, and healing of our minds and hearts. As educa-tor and theologian Neal Maxwell reminds us: "The rules of the emotional, spiritual and relational universe are as demanding as those of the physical universe. . . . The universe responds only to law. Man did not get to the moon with random trajectories and with each astronaut 'doing his own thing.' The price for reaching the moon was obedience to universal law." By changing how we think and under-standing the dynamics that actually govern and produce highest-level living, we open ourselves to significance, learning in turn the lesser ground that most improvement programs cover, the ground of success. Embracing the universal laws, we tap into our potential to achieve our desired results—a potential that is in you and me and working through us right now.

The Art of Significance in this sense isn't simply a personal trans-formation book; it's a leadership book for those who want to achieve game-changing results. We all know that extraordinary athletes step up their performance in the biggest games; we forget that they are able to do this because they step up their performance in practice, too. Winning isn't a sometimes thing; it's an all-the-time thing, and we can achieve such sustained high performance only as part of a passionate, soulful journey toward significance. Likewise, true lead-ers don't require a title. Leadership is not voted on or assigned. It is earned, and the way to earn it, at the very highest level, is by walking the path of significance—by realizing our best selves, helping others, giving back, taking the high road, and doing the right thing, even when it's hard or unpopular. What all of us really seek in a leader, as Ralph Waldo Emerson put it, is "someone who will inspire us to be what we know we could become."

Take a good look at yourself: Are you pushing yourself to the highest possible level? Or are you just getting by, embracing the norms of a mediocre, success-obsessed society? We've all grown up under different circumstances, faced a variety of challenges, and de-veloped certain values and characteristics, but one thing we share is our desire to know that we matter. We want our lives to count. And we *can* have them count. Now is the time to focus not on what's impressive, but on what's important. With these Twelve Laws, allow yourself to feel inspired to think differently, prepare differently, and perform differently. Why sacrifice your soul or confine your mind to the axioms of mere success? Paraphrasing the words of my old friend and former colleague Jim Rohn, "Successful people believe formal education will make you a living. Significant individuals know self-education will make you a fortune."

I have compiled this work as a poignant reminder that our primary purpose in life is to experience the full measure of our existence, to take our last breath in the euphoric state of significance, and as leaders, to grow more leaders among the members of our teams. With this book, it is my hope that by broadening our minds we can turn ourselves into things of beauty, make highest level leadership automatic, and become artists of being truly alive.

Welcome to the journey!

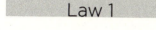

Practice Obedience Instead of Free Will Agency

The strongest is never strong enough to be always the master, unless he transforms strength into right, and obedience into duty.

—JEAN-JACQUES ROUSSEAU

Authorities who talk about being "great" or "best" usually affirm some notion of free will, asking us to consciously choose behaviors that ensure greatness. Successful entrepreneurs, coaches, athletes, civic leaders, parents, and students all hope to guarantee their success by pushing themselves of their own volition to do things they don't want to do in order to get the things that they want. At work, managers recognize star employees for purposely choosing to go above and beyond in the pursuit of excellence. Yet our freedom to choose, also commonly called "agency," is not the highest principle offering the path to true fulfillment and a meaningful life. *Obeying* entails an even higher, more universal law—one to which we will return throughout this book. When we grasp the concept of obedience in its five most important forms—humility, integrity, self-discipline, sacrifice, and order—we gain an essential understanding for doing what's necessary to be significant in any area of life.

Obedience is the universe's first law; all things revolve around obedience and are subject to it. As we see in the Jewish/Islamic/Christian tradition, people have sensed this since the beginning of recorded history—the biblical Adam, the first human creation, was held accountable for his obedience. With the whole world organized into a set of irrevocable laws, Adam and his posterity (us!) were given free will as a test of our obedience. As a constant source of positive influence to keep us strong we were also given what we commonly call our consciences.

We are all born into this world with an inherent sense of right and wrong. We naturally and automatically know we should be honest rather than dishonest, polite versus impolite, charitable instead of selfish. This sense of knowing corresponds to a set of basic universal laws—including the very Law of Obedience discussed in this chapter—granted us by a higher authority. When we obey a universal law, we glean specific rewards attached to that law, and when we disobey them, we suffer specific consequences. It's never about who is right but about *what* is right—and to achieve our greatest potential, we must always obey what we all, in the depths of our consciences, know to be right.

What is most unbelievable, however, is that most who disobey universal laws don't realize they are doing so. Disobedience may take many forms, including indifference toward life generally, lack of ambition, fear, or having an undefined purpose. Sometimes we are so ignorant of the laws that we attribute what happens to us not to law, but to luck. In reality, nature knows no such law as luck, or for that matter, coincidence. If you merely drift through life, thinking free will gives you the ability to do so, life pays you its own price, on its own terms. The non-drifter, however, who also exercises his or her agency, makes life pay on *his or her* own terms. Ultimately, luck has nothing to do with it.

Free will thus isn't quite as "free" as it seems—at least not from the point of view of significance. *The right to do something does not mean that doing it is right (or that it will bring results you'll like).* Without agency, we could not choose rightly and progress, yet with agency we can choose wrongly and fall short of our potential as human beings. Most good managers know that they cannot help their subordinates grow and excel unless they enable them to make decisions on their own. Such managers must also accept as part of the bargain that inexperienced employees might make *poor* decisions and obtain disappointing results.

Because of the way some use their agency, they lose their agency. When we don't obey universal laws or the specific rules that derive from them, our opportunities are reduced, and we fall captive to our choices—whether or not we realize it. However, when we do obey, our obedience ultimately protects our agency. Our right to order around a subordinate at work doesn't mean that this is the right thing to do, and, in fact, our rudeness will ultimately cost us their professionalism and respect. Conversely, for example, when we obey the rules of exercise and nutrition, we avoid the consequences of poor health, obesity, and addictions to substances that literally rob us of our ability to act for ourselves. When we obey the counsel to avoid debt and follow the rules of financial investing and savings, we use our agency and obtain the liberty to use our disposable income to help others.

In extolling obedience's virtues, I am not arguing it should *replace* free will or agency. As a vital preparatory law to the advanced, highest Law of Obedience, free will allows us to attain our best selves and reach the full measure of our existence. A man who behaves rightly because someone forces him to is demonstrably less significant than a man who *willingly chooses* to do right; we can improve ourselves only by actively choosing to stretch. Yet free will alone without an intention to obey universal laws gets us nowhere; as we've seen, we can *choose* to drift, to fail to meet our potential, and to surrender our freedom. To become significant, we must exercise our choice wisely to transcend ourselves and serve greater causes. Simply put: We must choose to obey. Obedience thus amounts to a broader, fuller expression of free will or agency. It is the highest universal law, whereas free will or agency is a necessary preparatory one. The more significant you are, the more obedient you become, but also, paradoxically, the more free.

Freedom to Obey

Let me say a bit more about this paradox. The concept of free will or agency presupposes a basic reality of the universe: The opposition in all things. Unless there is wrong, we have no right; without darkness, we cannot appreciate the light; without rain, we would not value sunshine; without falsehood, truth is not cherished; without death, life is not sacred and honored; without corruption, there can be no purity; without law, no justice; without punishment, no mercy; without wickedness, no happiness. We need both sides of the opposition in order to be able to choose to obey; otherwise, the choice would be meaningless. Likewise, we cannot expect to develop personality traits, character, leadership skills, and a special sense of self without experiencing grief, sorrow, pain, betrayal, and loneliness—in other words, opposition. (The path to significance is a hard process, indeed. If it was easy, everybody would achieve it. The hard is what makes it significant. However, it is simple, if we simply learn to obey.)

Champions realize the highest levels of freedom by freely choosing to obey higher rules and to do more than just what's best for the moment. When we are rewarded for an action, when we do the right thing, it is because we practiced self-mastery and obeyed the law that governs that action. When we do not achieve a specific desired result, when we do the wrong thing, it is because of disobedience to that specific law.

Philosophers have debated the relationship between agency and obedience for centuries. Some argue that in order to be morally responsible for some action, you must take that action freely. For example, if you see someone drowning in a lake, but you are tied to a stake in the ground and cannot free yourself, then you are not morally to blame for not rescuing the drowning swimmer. However, we can ask, "Why were you tied to the stake?" Most likely, if you had obeyed universal laws of right and wrong, you would not have lost your freedom and could have saved the swimmer. Our desires dictate our priorities, priorities shape our choices, and choices determine our actions. Shaping our desires and our actions in accordance with law causes us to become something—a true and trusted friend, a gifted mentor, or an exceptional human being who is always physically, mentally, morally, and emotionally ready to rescue lost and drowning souls.

Why a Kite Flies

To understand how the seemingly contradictory concepts of agency and obedience are really complementary, consider the story about a father and his young son who are flying a kite on a windy day. The dad asks the boy what holds up the kite in the sky. The boy answers, "The wind."

"No," the dad says, "the string."

The son shakes his head. "No, the string holds the kite down."

To which the father smiles and says, "If you think so, let go of the string."

The boy does so, and the kite flutters and falls to the ground. The boy is forced to chase the string all over the park. When he finally catches it and holds on tight, the kite immediately climbs back up to the reaches of the sky.

As the force of the air blows against the face of the kite, and as we hold on to the string, we create an equal and opposite force against the wind, and this force allows the kite to climb. If we disobey this law of opposition by letting go of the string, the kite does not work. The son quickly learns that rules don't hold us down; they allow us to control the actions and reactions in our lives, so that we can climb as high as we choose.

Tangentially, it may well be that parents' number one responsibility is to teach their children to obey. Children are naturally selfish; teaching them to obey entails not merely delivering lessons through kites, but teaching them why and how to *sacrifice*. Sadly, parents all too often confuse teaching obedience with controlling behavior. If children, athletes, and employees aren't taught to obey their leaders in the simple things, how in the world are they ever going to obey the other laws of the universe?

Five Faces of Character

Obedience produces significance by giving rise to a series of honorable traits that we associate with *character*. In describing character, Aristotle left us with his four virtues: wisdom, respect, courage, and moderation. Ancient Hebrew prophets such as Micah taught that we must have justice (integrity), mercy (kindness), and humility (meekness). Even the ancient Greeks discussed character. Whenever something happened, good or bad, the popular cry was "fate." The great philosophers rebutted this and proclaimed that character is destiny. Fate is when something happens to you over which you have no control. Destiny is when you decide to take control. Character in all these intellectual traditions, then, entails the reining in of our desires and impulses in accordance with an outside law. And that in turn involves five basic things—humility, integrity, self-discipline, sacrifice, and order—all of which constitute different sides of the more fundamental concept of obedience.

HUMILITY

The first side of character in obedience, *humility*, might lead to some initial confusion. Being humble doesn't mean that you are quiet, soft-spoken, self-deprecating, unassuming, less fortunate, or poor. Genuine humility entails being teachable and submissive—surrendering to the authority or control of another and/or yielding oneself to the will of a higher power. When training Secretariat, the greatest thoroughbred racehorse of all time, his handlers didn't break his spirit. They only broke him to the point of submissiveness, so that his talent and energy could be bridled and guided to help him reach his full potential. When we're humble, we retain strong affection for others, concern ourselves with their welfare, and find ourselves unselfishly devoted to something larger than ourselves.

INTEGRITY

We can define the second character in the obedience trait, *integrity*, as doing the right thing when people are watching, but more important, doing the right thing when they *aren't*.

I once took a five-hour flight from California to Florida and was in first class. I used the lavatory in that section of the plane. When I entered the tiny room and locked the door, I was blindsided by a gross, putrid, gooey, "mystery muck" snaking its way down the mirror. In addition, I found used paper towels on the sink, water splashed from corner to corner, and litter on the floor. When I stopped gagging, it occurred to me that the person who came in right after me would think that I did all this! I held my nose, cleaned it up, and finished my comfort break. Returning to my seat, I stared into the faces of the other twenty-three first-class passengers, silently asking, "Okay, which one of you low-budget slobs trashed this washroom?" I stared out the window to gain my composure, realizing an important life lesson: You cannot buy class—and class certainly entails the exercise of integrity. What a shame and a disgrace that so many think money and power make them somebody they are not! So, again, I ask, is it enough to be successful or should we always strive to be significant?

SELF-DISCIPLINE

To fully understand how critical integrity is to developing and maintaining character, and how it relates to character in obedience's third realm, *discipline,* consider a group of American pilots who were shot down and captured during the Vietnam War. Brigadier General Robinson Risner, Senator John McCain, Captain Charlie Plumb, and my dear friend Captain Gerry Coffee spent five to seven years in solitary confinement at the infamous North Vietcong Hoa Lo Prison (nicknamed the "Hanoi Hilton"). Each has told me that when he took off on that fateful day, he believed he possessed everything he needed to survive a disastrous situation as part of his uniform: helmet, gloves, steel-toed boots, protective flight suit, and a survival vest carefully stashed with a radio, a compass, a knife, flares, and a small-caliber handgun. However, when they were shot down and captured, their captors took all this away. If any man was to persevere and live, his strength had to come from within.

And so it did. Whenever one of them was dragged from his cell for interrogation, his rallying cry was "RWH"—Return With Honor—knowing that returning to his cell and eventually to his beloved United States of America would mean nothing unless he had been true to himself and obeyed his core values. On a good day, each prisoner had three cups of water to take a bath. On a good day, each prisoner had food. On a good day, the tapping sounds, the flapping towels, the scraping rakes, and swishing brooms they used for communication made sense and were understood.

On the bad days, the guards beat them—and then some. I have visited this same North Vietnamese Hoa Lo Prison and have seen firsthand where our men were brutally tortured beyond comprehension. The pressure to sell out was continuous and unrelenting. Some would sit in solitary confinement, starving and deteriorating. Others were locked in rusted iron stockades, which contorted them into unnatural positions. Many died. Those who followed the Code of Conduct, those with courage, those disciplined enough to uphold the chain of command, watched as others who could not—who would not—walked away and were released from the camps.

These POWs survived their unimaginable ordeal because of their self-discipline. In his own words, Captain Coffee told me, "It wasn't what I had on me, but what I had *in* me, that sustained me through the brutal beatings, bone dislocations, attempted brain washing, and long separation from loved ones. I survived and lived to tell about it because I had self-discipline that strengthened me to obey my conscience, obey my instincts, and obey my commitment to defend and represent my country and the freedoms we believe in through sacrifice with courage!"

SACRIFICE

Self-discipline leads us inexorably to the concept of *sacrifice*. To sacrifice is to relinquish something valuable or precious, often so as to accomplish a greater purpose. In baseball, the sacrifice bunt is a strategy whereby a batter seeks to advance a teammate who is on base by willingly forgoing the batter's own chance to safely make a base hit. Sacrifice allows us to learn something about ourselves and distinguishes us from the rest of the world. It also is intimately bound up with the concept of obedience.

In ancient times, certain religious traditions required their followers to offer up animal sacrifices to their god. In modern times, we shift the focus of the sacrifice from a person's animal to the person himself. Neal Maxwell said, "This higher practice of obedience through sacrifice reaches into the inner soul of a person. Real, personal sacrifice never was placing an animal on the altar. Instead, it is a willingness to put the animal in us upon the altar and letting it be consumed!" Only when we overcome our own selfish desires can we live the law of obedience. The spirit of sacrifice humbles us to obey and promotes gratitude.

Ours has been a period of great prosperity that may, when history is written, prove to be as devastating to our souls as are the effects of physical persecutions. I fear that the principle of sacrifice may be slipping away from us. If life becomes too easy, we take for granted what matters most, stop looking at ourselves as *the* competition, and we lose our "eye of the tiger" that placed us on top in the first place. Do you know people who constantly try to live off of their past laurels while complaining they're bored? What they are really confessing is that *they* are boring! They expect life to entertain them, and consequently they kick back waiting for life to happen. I often see this in small-town USA. When I ask a small-town teenager if he likes it there, he usually replies, "No, there is nothing to do." Where did he get the convoluted idea that his community bears responsibility to make his life exciting? In the corporate world, way too many people hate their jobs, only looking forward to Friday instead of Monday, and thinking that they are paid by the hour; in reality, they are paid *for the value that they bring* to that hour.

In thinking about sacrifice, we must acknowledge that the value of something is determined by what we are willing to surrender to obtain it. In our universe governed by moral law, we can choose success and get what we want right now and then pay for it afterward, or we can choose significance and pay for it first, before we get it.

Years ago, I attended a company retreat featuring a famous comedian hired by the organizers at extraordinary expense. I sat at the head table with the chairman, president of the organization, and other senior executives. As the program began, I realized that the entertainer's idea of humor was vulgarity, profanity, and borderline racism. The performance made me so uncomfortable that I thought about leaving, yet I worried that the executives and board members would take my departure as a statement of disrespect and prudishness. After a few more minutes of internal debate, I got up and left. This monumental moment allowed me to experience the exhilarating self-esteem building and confidence strengthening that comes when we actually obey a higher law, especially when our actions are unpopular and nonconformist. When we are hard on ourselves, life is easy. When we are easy on ourselves, life is hard. *We can choose to be an inspirational example or a horrible warning.*

On the surface, exiting the corporate show might have seemed to reflect shallow intolerance on my part. But as you will discover in Law 9, tolerance is only a lesser law of success that perpetuates prejudice and quiet bigotry. Acceptance is the highest law, beginning and sustaining itself with the understanding that when our deepest beliefs diverge from our actions, we will never feel truly happy or live in the highest realm of self-actualization called significance. We can fool others, but we can never fool ourselves!

ORDER

When we practice humility, integrity, self-discipline, and self-sacrifice, we follow regimens that generate *order* in our lives—the fifth face of character required of obedience. These regimens are concrete, clear, intelligent, and rigorously pursued performance mechanisms that keep us on track. Some call these regimens righteous routines; others look at them as iron rods that they can hold on to that will take them from where they are to where they want to be. Personally, I call these routines patterns—and I am deliberate about that language. Routines and rods are man-made systems based on who is right. It's, "You do this because I said so," regardless of whether the routine is good, better, great, best, or right. The patterns I'm speaking of already exist in the universe. Based on *what* is right, on conscience, they give us quick and constant access to the universe's governing powers.

Patterns exist for becoming an exemplary leader or a competent mother; for increasing sales or for creating extraordinary customer experiences; for winning a political election; or for accomplishing an array of other goals. Those who discover the patterns simplify every

process, increase productivity, and attain results quicker. The following exercise will prove this:

Time yourself for one minute and see how many numbers you can
find in sequential order starting with the number 1. Find 2, then 3, 4,
5, and so on until you have located all 90 numbers.

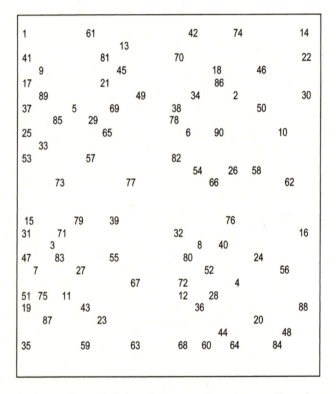

How many numbers did you locate? Below is a replica chart that
has been divided into four quadrants. Once you figure out the orderly pattern that was used to create the chart, your speed, efficiency,
and effectiveness in finding the numbers skyrockets. Starting in

the upper left box, locate the number 1. In the upper right box is number 2. In the lower left box is number 3. In the lower right box is number 4. Back up to the upper left box you'll find number 5, and so on. Time yourself again for one minute and compare your scores.

```
1           61                    42        74            14
                 13
41              81           70                           22
     9              45                   18      46
17              21                       86
     89             49           34      2              30
37      5    69              38                  50
     85   29                 78
25              65               6    90            10
     33                      82
53          57                     54    26  58
        73          77                 66              62
---------------------------------------------------------------
15        79    39                           76
31     71                    32                          16
    3                               8    40
47     83        55          80                  24
   7       27                      52              56
                    67       72          4
51  75   11                  12      28
19             43                  36                     88
     87         23                               20
                                       44        48
35          59        63     68    60    64      84
```

Let's now look at some examples of orderly patterns in our daily life. In the business world, entrepreneurs must strictly abide by four rules:

1. Above all, have a product or service that is better than anyone else's. Otherwise you end up with a mere commodity.

2. Hire and train good people, maintaining an effective sales force. Sales are everybody's business, and customer service is not a department—it's an attitude. Disobey this rule and profitability needs go unmet.

3. Have adequate financial backing, liquidity, lines of credit, and inventory. Disobey this rule and you are out of cash and business.

4. Always know whom you are dealing with. Otherwise you lose personally and professionally. There's a difference between trusting a brand's quality and reputation and trusting the person who owns the shop where you buy the brand.

Other business patterns that provide order are not hard to find. In the world of real estate, for example, champion realtors obey a regimen that includes routinely telephoning twenty former clients; phoning all the FSBO properties (For Sale By Owner) in their working area and asking for a chance to meet with them; and sending every person on their mailing list a quarterly newsletter.

As a professional speaker, I have devised my own orderly pattern: I always write a story, let it sit for a day, rewrite it so every word "pays its own way," and then practice telling it ten times before I ever use it in a speech. Patterns such as these help generate conventional success, but humility, integrity, self-discipline, sacrifice, and order together constitute true character—the inner source and manifestation of our capacity to obey.

Perfect Practice Makes Permanent

To understand how the five faces of character/obedience lead to significance, let's turn to sports. Champion athletes must obey strict training rules and relentlessly prepare in a practice environment before they can compete at the highest level of competition. Wayne Gretzky, affectionately called "The Great One," is the greatest hockey player to ever have played the game. With his ability to influence the lives of so many young hockey players and fans, he clearly has attained significance. The greatest single influence in Wayne's life, however, is another significant man—his father, Walter. Walt was his coach and mentor, and he has always been and always will be his best friend. Wayne considers his greatest honor, what he most respects about his identity, is when he is introduced as Walter Gretzky's son.

I had the honor of talking with Wayne, but I took special pleasure spending two days with Walter in his home in Brantford, Ontario, Canada. We played golf and laughed; toured his famous basement full of Wayne's MVP awards, trophies, autographed sticks, skates, and jerseys; laughed some more; and swapped inspirational stories. Walt is smart and intense, yet also warm and engaging. He is a deeply committed family man, yet community oriented in his tireless efforts toward charitable organizations. Even in his twilight years, Walt coached junior hockey teams and helped hundreds of young people. Wayne is famous for answering the question *Why are you the greatest player?* with the highly quoted response, "Most players go where the puck is; I go to where the puck is going to be." According to Walt, Wayne's ability to anticipate the puck's future location testified to his strict, selfless, and humble obedience to the process of preparation, even, and especially, when others weren't looking.

If you wanted to discover why Wayne was the greatest hockey player who ever lived, you didn't watch him on the ice; you watched him when he was on the bench. He studied every player to see where he went, how he passed, to whom he passed, which side he favored, whether he skated better to the left or to the right, how he defended going backward, and who his favorite partner was in certain playmaking situations. By the time Wayne hit the ice, he knew exactly where to go to intercept a pass or to block a shot, and when to skate into the lanes of the other team to shoot and score. Preparation—doing the hard work even when he himself didn't feel it was in him—is why Wayne Gretzky is hockey's all-time leading scorer.

According to Walt, Wayne is a perfectionist who used to practice the same shot from the same place on the ice hundreds of times an afternoon. When most kids lost interest and concentration, Wayne somehow kicked it into a higher gear and endured until he succeeded at what he was trying to accomplish. He even practiced hitting the puck off certain places in the hockey rink baseboards so he would know exactly where the puck would go when it ricocheted. Wayne's capacity to prepare was so intense that he persuaded his dad to build a hockey rink in the backyard so he could practice at the crack of dawn and continue until neighbors complained late at night about the noise. The only thing that took Wayne off the ice was his dad's reminder that he needed to go to bed and rest so he could wake up refreshed, alert, and ready to do it again. Ironically, the thing that made Wayne the greatest hockey player ever and a great sports celebrity philanthropist was his dad Walter's constant reminder to always

be prepared: physically, mentally, emotionally, socially, and financially. Walter taught Wayne that humility, integrity, discipline, sacrifice, and order can lead us to a life worth living—both on and off the
"ice rink" of life.

The No Excuses Leadership School

To cap our discussion of the highest Universal Law of Obedience, I
again draw your attention to the U.S. military, specifically the elite
few known as the Army Rangers, who along with the Navy SEALs (as
in Team 6, who killed Osama bin Laden), Delta Force, and the Special Forces Green Berets constitute the world's most highly trained
and feared warriors. The Ranger Creed illustrates what all these special men share in common: a nearly incomprehensible obedience, an
unselfish commitment to duty, to honor, to country, to one another,
and to service before self. As you read, ask yourself if you are man or
woman enough to hold yourself to this same high standard of ethical excellence in all you do, and if that level of ethical excellence exists within your organization.

My young neighbor, U.S. Army Lieutenant and Scout Platoon
Leader Ben Westman (whom I coached in football for six years),
graduated from the U.S. Military Academy at West Point, serving in
his senior year as one of only thirty-two company commanders. After graduation, Ben headed for the fifty-six-day, intensely grueling
Ranger School, affectionately called "No Excuses Leadership Training." Each day, candidates spend long hours hiking, running, and
swimming in full combat gear. They sleep in the field and eat two
meals less a day than normal, losing twenty to thirty pounds by the

time the training concludes. Although most candidates don't make it through this school on their first attempt, Ben passed with flying colors and upon graduation proudly committed to obey the Ranger Creed.

THE UNITED STATES ARMY RANGER CREED

Recognizing that I volunteered as a Ranger, fully knowing the hazards of my chosen profession, I will always endeavor to uphold the prestige, honor, and high esprit-de-corps of my Rangers Regiment.

Acknowledging the fact that a Ranger is a more elite Soldier who arrives at the cutting edge of battle by land, sea, or air, I accept the fact that as a Ranger my country expects me to move further, faster, and fight harder than any other Soldier.

Never shall I fail my comrades. I will always keep myself mentally alert, physically strong, and morally straight, and I will shoulder more than my share of the task, whatever it may be, one hundred percent and then some.

Gallantly will I show the world that I am a specially selected and well-trained Soldier. My courtesy to superior officers, neatness of dress, and care of equipment shall set the example for others to follow.

Energetically will I meet the enemies of my country. I shall defeat them on the field of battle for I am better trained and will fight with all my might. Surrender is not a Ranger word. I will never leave a fallen comrade to fall into the hands of the enemy and under no circumstances will I ever embarrass my country.

> **R**eadily will I display the intestinal fortitude required to
> fight on to the Ranger objective and complete the mission,
> though I be the lone survivor.

These are not mere words. Ben is now leading and fighting side by side with his men in the mountains of Afghanistan. The last time I saw Ben, he left me with his proud and intense war call, "Rangers Lead the Way," and a quote by Steven Pressfield that gave me a greater sense of how Rangers think, feel, prepare, and thrive in their high-performance world: "When a warrior fights not for himself, but for his brothers; when his most passionately sought goal is neither glory nor his own life's preservation, but to spend his substance for them, his comrades; not to abandon them, not to prove unworthy of them; then his heart has truly achieved contempt for death; and with that he transcends himself and his actions touch the sublime."

I witnessed this highest level of service before self during one of my many visits to Landstuhl Regional Medical Center in Germany. Joining doctors on their rounds, I visited with an army sergeant who had lost a leg and an arm in an IED explosion. He had been in the hospital five days and was traveling that morning back to the United States for additional specialized care. As my hosts and I approached the bed of this brave soldier, he raised his one good arm up in the air. "Hey, Doc, look, I'm still useful. I can still fight. I heard they're sending me back to the States, but you can't! Any of my brothers here? You gotta help me stay with my guys in Kandahar." With tears in his eyes he pleaded, "Please don't take me away from my men."

All specialized weapons, survival, and combat-readiness programs require and instill extreme fitness, yet these elite fighting men realize a greater purpose and a more comprehensive residual benefit while pushing themselves to their ultimate capacity and potential. As a candidate graduates, he is sworn in with an unshakeable commitment to integrity, loyalty, and excellence in all he does. What creeds do you have in your organization to inspire this level of sacrifice, unity, hard work, and love? Jim Rohn taught me, "Life responds to *deserve* and not to *need*. It doesn't say, 'If you *need*, you will reap.' It says, 'If you *plant*, you will reap.'" Does your culture provide rigorous training that instills values and builds character? If you don't yet possess the structure of obedience, isn't it time to sit down and create one?

The Bottom Line

We like to see free will and obedience as opposites, but, in fact, they're not. Free will is the preparatory law, while obedience—which requires and presumes free will—leads us to significance. We may be free to choose for ourselves, but we are not free to choose the consequence of our actions. When we make a choice, we receive the specific consequence of that choice. Practicing obedience means freely choosing to learn what we need to learn, do what we need to do, and be the significant being we need to be, when we need to be it. In order for any of us to want what we get and reach the highest level of leadership and living, we must identify the laws that, when obeyed, will yield our desired results, and then, and most important, we must actually do the things that others are not willing to do.

Four Suggested Action Steps to Learning Obedience

1. Create personal vision, mission, and values statements. Vision articulates your purpose, outlining what you do and why you do it. Mission specifies your tactical priorities, describing how and when you do things. Values such as duty, honor, integrity, service before self, excellence in all you do, compassion, respect, accountability, teamwork, and expertise define your character and what you stand for. They highlight what matters most to you and describe the collective principles and ideals that guide your decisions and actions.

2. Think of an area in which you want to excel. Identify a guru or a mentor who has done what you want to do. Obtain his or her detailed description of exactly what, why, and how he or she accomplished the goal. Gathering strength from your vision, mission, and values statements, take action on your mentor's plan. Keep it simple. Work and relentlessly obey for short periods of time. Performing easy exercises broken down into smaller increments one at a time is simpler and more helpful than learning a whole exercise in one sitting. Perform an exercise for as many times as it takes to get it right. Once you get it right, stop and reward yourself. As you continue, you will learn to duplicate the correct action faster in order to reap your rewards more quickly.

3. In both your personal and professional lives, commit to noticing each and every day a person who has gone to great lengths to do something noble, even when no one was looking. Go out

of your way to compliment this person on what you noticed. That evening, take time to write a short note reiterating how significant you thought this person's behavior was. Also, help your organization catch others doing honorable things. Create a collection box where coworkers can submit positive notes about one another. Ask your boss to create a monthly meeting to acknowledge extraordinary acts. Guaranteed, in three to four weeks you will have improved the quality of your own behavior, and you will in turn have inspired others to do the same.

4. In addition to your personal vision, mission, and value statements, create a personal credo written in the first person, similar to the previously quoted Ranger Creed. Let one of my favorite sayings inspire you: "I am only one. But I am one. I can't do everything, but I can do something. That which I can do I ought to do. That which I ought to do, by grace I shall do." When you've written your creed, frame it, display it, obey it!

Exercise Perseverance Instead of Patience

Endurance is not just the ability to bear a hard thing, but to turn it into glory.

—WILLIAM BARCLAY

Just as free will serves as a lesser, preparatory law to obedience, so, too, does the much-lauded notion of patience serve as but a prelude to the advanced, highest Universal Law of Perseverance. Patience and perseverance might seem similar, but they're, in fact, quite different. Patience denotes passive, mindless endurance of a hardship. This is a good start, but perseverance goes further, suggesting our *active, mindful embrace* of hardship in service of a higher goal or purpose. Patience is morally and spiritually neutral, while perseverance is meaningful and always connected to broader awareness, intent, and devotion. It entails an understanding not merely of the how, but of the why.

Patience may be a virtue, as we have all been taught, but any virtue, when taken to an extreme, can become a vice. Limited to the idea of mindless endurance, patience gives us an excuse never to begin, saying, in effect, "Wait your turn!" With the higher awareness implied by perseverance, we've already *made* our decision and are *taking* our turn, in that we've committed ourselves to a higher purpose and are moving little by little and out of our own volition toward significance. Perseverance represents mind over matter in the deepest sense, reflecting our thoughtful resolution that we will "happen" to life, not merely allow life to "happen" to us. To transform ourselves from successful to significant, we must make the mind run the body and always tell the body what to do.

The Law of Perseverance naturally accompanies that of Obedience. We might commit to living the first law of the universe, but it is only through mastery of this second and sequential law that we will constantly and consistently see it through. Most people selectively obey structures—whether the foundational universal laws or the more specific rules and regulations of mundane life—only when convenient. On every flight on every airline in the world, flight attendants tell us to always keep our seatbelts fastened. When we finally receive permission to get up to use the facilities, we are instructed to immediately return to our seats and loosely fasten our seatbelts again. How many passengers selectively obey? We must remember that *all* rules and laws—including mundane ones—exist for a reason. On April 4, 2012, the *Houston Chronicle* reported that 12 passengers were injured on a United Airlines flight that encountered "strong turbulence somewhere over Louisiana." Footage from Houston's local news station KTRK showed passengers taken from the plane in stretchers—some in neck braces—to waiting ambulances.

Had these 12 simply persevered in their obedience like the other 145 passengers, they would have avoided injury.

Plodding Along, Finding Our Way

One practical problem with patience is that it usually proves weaker than perseverance. Sure, we might endure pain for a while, but lacking a deeper awareness of why we're enduring, we eventually become distracted and overwhelmed; we allow the emotional "weather" around us to affect our attitudes and resolve. The higher awareness of perseverance fortifies us to stay determined, to stay on task, and to believe that everything will be fine in the end—because if it's not okay, it's not the end! Think of your own life and how much easier it is to discipline yourself, make sacrifices, and pursue difficult goals when you're conscious at every moment of why you're doing what it is you are doing.

Staying the course no matter what is so critical, as progress can often occur after most people might have given up hope. When you plant a Chinese bamboo tree, water it, and fertilize it, nothing happens for the first year. There's no sign of growth. The same thing happens—or doesn't happen—the second year. The tree is continually watered and fertilized each year, but nothing shows for eight years. Suddenly, in the ninth year it grows thirty-nine inches in twenty-four hours and continues this growth spurt until it reaches its full height of ninety-eight feet and a diameter of eight inches in just one hundred days. What would have happened if we'd given up in the first year, or even after eight years?

Significance brings glory, to borrow theologian William Barclay's word, but the actual practice of significance is a daily slog, a faithful and mindful plodding driven by our love for what we are doing and the cherished dreams that follow from and reflect that love. Major League Hall of Famer Cal Ripken Jr., nicknamed "Ironman" because he started and played in 2,632 consecutive games over 17 seasons, didn't set out to establish this incredible record. He simply worked hard every day at what he loved—at every practice, at every game— and the record set itself. Indeed, this was patience—but so much more: With a keen awareness of his purpose, of his sense of the why, he *persevered*!

I can't guarantee that your mindful plodding on the job or in your daily life will yield the exact rewards you envision, but I will say this: We never really know what can happen, so we can't quit—it's a league rule! I was once on a program with Henry Winkler—the "Fonz" from the old television sitcom *Happy Days*. Henry decided to take time off and treat himself to a matinee movie. To avoid having fans fuss over him, he entered the theater from the side door. As he sat down, a little girl in the row behind him smiled, pointed her finger, and slowly said, "Fonzie." Winkler snapped into the Fonzie character, flipping his hair, swiveling his hips, and glancing left and right. In his signature pose, he pointed his finger at the girl and said, "Hey! Whoa!" To everyone's surprise, the lady sitting next to the little girl passed out. The theater manager came in to assist the woman who was now lying in the aisle and put a cold pack on her forehead. "Why did you pass out?" he asked.

Pointing to the little girl, she replied, "My daughter's autistic, and that is the very first word she has ever spoken in her entire life!"

It turns out the doctors had told this mother that her little angel would never be able to talk. But because of this mother's constant awareness of her higher purpose—making the best possible life for her daughter—she had gone the extra mile and taken her little girl to the finest therapists, hoping to help her at least understand the mechanics of speaking in case something clicked at some point in her life. If this mother had merely been patient, she likely would have fallen prey to insecurity and despair, welcoming the rationalization that we can do tomorrow what we should do today. She would never have endured to experience this wonderful moment of hearing her daughter finally speak.

One Moment at a Time

Turning success into significance is not an intricate, drawn-out process of learning esoteric new habits and following a magical ten-step program. It's simpler than that, beginning with awareness of a purpose and continuing with an unwavering, intentional commitment to obey universal laws. Significant people obey *right now*. And they accomplish their daily routines by focusing on the only thing that really matters—the present moment.

Dan Jansen won the gold medal in the 1000-meter event at the 1994 Olympic Games in Lillehammer, Norway. It was a long time in coming. In 1984 he competed at the Olympics in Sarajevo, Yugoslavia, placing fourth in the 500-meter race and sixteenth in the 1000-meter race. At the 1988 Olympics in Calgary, Canada, he fell during the 500- and 1000-meter races and failed to finish. In 1992, at Albertville, France, he placed fourth in the 500-meter and an embarrassing twenty-sixth in the 1000-meter. Despite these disappointments, Jansen continued to persevere, retaining his place on the U.S. Olympic team for the 1994 games. In the 500-meter race, he slipped momentarily, avoiding a fall but losing enough time to finish in eighth place. In the 1000-meter race, his last Olympic event and his last race ever, Jansen finally won a gold medal, establishing a world-record time of 1:12.43.

An interview with Jansen's coach, Dr. Jim Loehr, revealed how he persevered to finally win the elusive gold. Loehr said he simply coached Dan to develop an emotional focus on the moment. Technically, it was "one foot in front of the other." Mentally, it was to "maintain feelings of gratitude for all the years the sport had given him." During lengthy talks, Dr. Loehr convinced Dan that thinking about its being his last race, his final opportunity to win an Olympic medal, was counterproductive and would drain his energy and distract from his focus. To persevere, our technical "one thing" and our personal "one thing" need to fuse to produce a focus on being in the moment. Forget about the future and the past: The only thing that matters is the one moment in time—and then the next one moment in time. Perseverance, indeed, becomes simple (although not easy!) when we block out all distractions, avoid the paralysis of thinking too much, and focus all our concentrated energy and emotion on the task at hand.

"She Could Have Died"

Although daily, ongoing struggle defines the route to significance, the path comes laden with pivotal, make-or-break moments, times of crisis that establish just how much character we really possess and just how dedicated we are to our underlying purpose. Here mere seekers of success turn around and go home, their patience at an end. The significant person perseveres because she treats such moments as an opportunity to rededicate herself on an even deeper level to her higher purpose or goal.

My daughter Nikola began competing as a gymnast at the age of four under the tutelage of renowned gymnastics coaches Missy Marlowe (a member of the 1988 U.S. Olympic Team) and Dave Hancock. On one occasion when Nikola was twelve, she was performing her routine on the uneven parallel bars, spinning around, alternating from the top to the bottom bar, letting go as she flew and somersaulted from one bar to the other and back again in pointed spread-eagle form. The end of her routine called for Nikola to spin twice around the top bar in a maneuver known as the Giant-Giant Fly Away, catapulting into a backflip in pike position to stick her landing on the mat. As I stood in the balcony watching, she rotated the last time, and her hands slipped off the bar and she slammed to the ground, landing on her neck. A collective gasp filled the gym as coaches rushed to her aid. She was unconscious. After making my way to the floor, we took her to the emergency room. A CAT scan and an MRI revealed a stretched A-LAR ligament in her neck. Before Nikola was released, her physical therapist told us, "She could have died."

If you were her parent, what would you have Nikola do? The best thing would have been to have her quit gymnastics, baby her body for the rest of the year, and feel grateful she wasn't paralyzed. Despite having suffered a career-ending football injury myself, I maintained (and my wife concurred) that the *right* thing was to make sure Nikola did not deviate from adhering to the inwardly defined purpose she had followed throughout her gymnastics career. If this purpose had sustained her when things were going good, it should be even more important to believe in and follow when things went bad.

A bit of extra background: From the time Nikola and our other kids were small, I had them repeat the "Clark Credo" every night before they went to bed. This credo, created by my wife and me, states:

> I'm smart, talented, and I never say never. I'm wanted, important, loveable, capable, and I can succeed. I'm coordinated, I love music, and I'm going to get good grades in school. If I fail or fall down, I just get back up and go again. If I spill or make a mistake, I just clean it up, learn why, and say, No big deal. I will always do the right thing simply because it's the right thing to do, and make everybody around me better—especially my family, because families are forever!

As our kids grew older and could finally understand what all the words meant and how positive thinking really does make a difference in every situation, the philosophies expressed in this credo became part of their automatic thought processes. This strengthened their support system, especially in times of trial and error when they needed it most.

No surprise, then: Nikola decided to continue with gymnastics. After six weeks out of the gym, she returned for conditioning. No, we are not psycho parents who expected it. Nikola returned because she knew what she was doing and demanded it of herself. All our children have been raised to believe that we don't measure people when they are up, we measure them when they are down. As our motto goes, get knocked down seven times, get up eight.

It took time for Nikola to face her fears and work herself back into shape, but five months after her scary crash, she competed in her first meet. That year, she went on to be crowned State Level Six Champion in both floor exercise and balance beam, and placed second in the all-around competition. I'll never forget the look in her eyes at the state championship and the expression on the faces of her coaches and teammates when it was her turn to compete on the uneven bars. Taking a deep breath, thirteen-year-old Nikola did the right thing, climbed up on the bars, and performed her routine. We all held our breath when she got to the end and started into her Giants. I can't imagine what went through her mind as she spun and released to soar through the air into the same pike position backflip. She stuck it! She did it! And because she chose to do the harder "right" instead of the easier "best," this single episode changed her perspective on what it takes for her to become all she was born to be.

What Nikola did on the gymnastics floor ultimately isn't what made her a champion. She became a champion because she made winning personal, realizing that losing hurts worse than winning feels good, and understanding that the highest purpose here is ultimately growth and self-actualization. She internalized the notion that pain is a signal to grow, not to suffer. Once we learn the lesson that pain is teaching us, the pain goes away. Through her trials and tribulations, Nikola learned obedience and perseverance; realized that failure is an event, not a person; and, in the process, became the master of her fate and the captain of her soul! This, in turn, was the beginning of her life of significance, which she has used to serve severely challenged children as a special education teacher. Is there any clear reason why you could not persevere in your own struggles and become more of who you already are, thus helping others become more of who they are?

The Bottom Line

You have never been this old before, and today, you will never be this young again. So right now matters. Perseverance at its core rests on identifying and pursuing our personal priorities *in the moment*. It's not just about staying in the game—that's mere patience. It's about staying in the game *and remaining aware of why you're doing it, what higher purpose you're trying to serve*. Plod along and never give up, knowing that when you reach those crisis points, you'll rise to the occasion.

Four Suggested Action Steps to Learning Perseverance

1. Make a comprehensive list of everything you are thankful for, and based on your talents and abilities, visualize what you are charged with mastering and accomplishing (remembering that where much is given, much is required). Document the total long-range impact of your proposed endeavors, and honestly and completely answer why you should do them.

2. Many don't recognize the full power of self-suggestion. If you believe that it can be done, and minimize risk through prepa-

ration, it surely *will* be done—one step at a time and one day at a time. Create an itemized plan with a timeline of preparation checkpoints. As a setback arises, do not dwell on it as a failure; rather, regard it as a teaching moment of what doesn't work, a stepping-stone to your goals. In life, there are no mistakes, only lessons.

3. Work around obstacles. If a task seems unmanageable at the outset, break it into smaller achievable goals. If you're learning to swim, celebrate at each accomplishment as you learn to float, breathe, do proper kicks, and execute smooth, rhythmic arm movements. Then end with a grand finale when the whole task is achieved. Remember, many of life's failures accrue to people who did not realize how close they were to success—and even significance—before they gave up.

4. Make a list of at least three people who have accomplished exactly what you are attempting to achieve. Research the details of their initial plans and document each of the obstacles and setbacks they encountered and what they did to overcome them. Become familiar with their successes and start visualizing the celebration you are going to have when you do what they did.

Proactively Stretch Instead of Change

Don't wish it was easier; wish you were better. . . . If you are not willing to risk the unusual, you will have to settle for the ordinary. The few who do are the envy of the many who only watch.

—JIM ROHN

Change, we're told, is good. Maybe—if mere success is all you want. To push ourselves further down the path to significance, we need to go beyond the preparatory principle of change and embrace a higher, more comprehensive law, that of *stretch*.

Successful people often observe that the only constant in life is change. I disagree. What we see around us virtually all the time is a *refusal* or *reluctance* to change. So many people fail because they can't change the bad habits that stymie them. Successful people have managed some change, but they progress only up to a point—and then they stop and stagnate. Why? Don't they have the talent and the smarts? Aren't they often in the right place at the right time? Their problem is they lack an *internal* drive to surpass themselves and become all they can be. Content with success, they would rather remain in the realm of the "impressive" known rather than venture into the "important" but riskier realm of the unknown. Not realizing that great is not good enough, they refuse to go beyond change and embrace stretch, a deeper, more personal, more meaningful process of development and growth.

You've heard the decades-old cliché to "think outside the box." Mere change is foisted upon us from outside; we react to the demands of others, including bosses, parents, and coaches. Stretch, by contrast, follows from our own heartfelt commitment to become more of who we already are—everything we have the potential to be, both personally and organizationally. That's right, the way to grow and prosper is to think *inside* the box! When we stretch, we change because *we* want to, because it's meaningful to *us*, because our *own* purposes require us to. Only because we proceed on our own initiative can we embrace the risk required to go beyond our present comfort level, achieve extreme levels of performance, and become significant.

To understand more precisely how stretch surpasses mere change in the process of personal growth, consider the following four-part matrix:

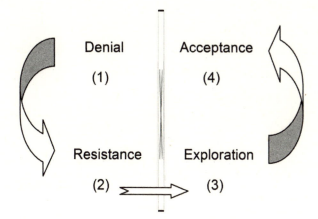

Change is usually forced on us in an atmosphere of organizational pressure and deadlines. Worse still, when your boss asks you to change, it feels as though he's asking you to admit that you have not been everything you could have been, or that you have been doing something insufficiently or wrong. Because none of us wants to admit this, we get caught up in denying the need for change and resisting the change. We fall into a victim's mentality, thinking, *Oh, no, now what? Why do I have to change? It's not fair and it's not my fault!* On occasions when we do eventually manage to change, it's because we're more or less yanked or pushed unpleasantly through the explore stage to acceptance. How many of us want to go through that process again?

Stretch, by contrast, is empowering from start to finish (and we're never finished!). It upholds the sense described in previous chapters that we are masters of our own destiny, individuals capable of injecting our own, "inside the box" meaning onto the world and inspiring others to do the same. At the moment we decide to change because *we* say so—because we have determined why, when, where, and how—resistance melts away. We suddenly *want* to explore all the benefits that will come of growth and we fully accept the challenge of stretching toward significance. Free-flowing movement from change and resistance into exploration and then acceptance comes only when we take action because we decide to—in other words, when we're stretching.

Lessons from the Physical Therapist

You may think that stretch, being internally driven, is a solitary process. Not true! Although deciding to stretch is a personal decision, we can stretch ourselves only so far on our own; in order to reach our ultimate capacity and potential as human beings, we need help.

Once I snapped my Achilles tendon playing basketball with the guys on my street. My ankle required surgery, and I was put in a plaster cast for three months. To fully recover, I underwent four weeks of physical therapy. In each session, the first thing the therapist did was warm up my stiff, weakened ankle. Then she took the tip of my foot and bent it and stretched it to a place it had never been. As I gritted my teeth and reminded myself that pain is temporary but quitting lasts forever, she then let go, and my foot flipped back to the same place it was before she started to stretch it. Isn't this the usual outcome of company sales rallies and corporate training where we get pumped up, but then leave and flip on back to the same old attitude and behavior we brought to the meeting?

Stretching requires that someone not merely take us past the point of discomfort, but support us as we hold ourselves in a zone of discomfort so that we can strengthen ourselves. Consider the Vertical Stretching Scale on the next page.

Obviously, the first step is to start where we are. Next, we push and strain ourselves to the point of discomfort. Third, we ask someone we trust and respect to stretch us past the point of discomfort and support us there until the strain and stretch are no longer stressful. Once we have grown comfortable at the 7, 8, or 9 levels, those become our new starting points, the new normal, and on our revised, amped-up scale we start again at 1. Now the level that used to be 10 becomes level 6—no longer the snapping point, but instead the targeted point of discomfort—which we now can handle and surpass with support.

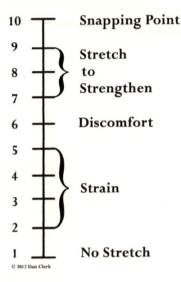

Too many of us want to stretch and strengthen all at once. Leaders set outrageously high, unrealistic goals without giving even a modest amount of support. Then they blame their people when they snap and fall. I know a lot of superstar athletes, corporate executives, military leaders, and professionals in every field who will verify that all strengthening occurs in the area past the point of discomfort. While you can get to the point of discomfort on your own, you need someone else whom you admire and respect to push you past discomfort and then support you there while you strengthen. If you're a manager, now is the time to ask yourself just what are you demanding of your people. Do they realistically have what they need from you to grow? Or are you just setting them up to snap right back to where they were the minute you, as the "physical therapist," stop exerting pressure?

The Broomstick Test

A great illustration of the kind of support we need in order to stretch is what I call the "broomstick test." When I work with professional or amateur athletic teams, I'll often assemble the team in their meeting room and ask a captain and an assistant coach to come to the front of the room and hold the ends of a broomstick so it is suspended twelve inches off the floor. Ahead of time, I get the name of the premier stud athlete on the team (the one with the thirty-eight-inch vertical leap), and when the broomstick is in place, I ask him to come forward and jump over the bar. I usually find him sitting in the back of the room, and he always hesitates and gives me a cocky, arrogant look, like, *Hey, don't you read the newspaper? Don't you know who I am? Why are you bugging me?*

After some prodding, he finally strolls up to the front of the room, walking with a swag that looks as though he had sat on something hot. I then ask him if he thinks he can jump over the twelve-inch-high broomstick. After he glares at me, conveying that this is a waste of his precious time and how dare I insult his athletic sophistication, I ask point-blank, "Will you jump over the broomstick?" Grinning sarcastically, he skips over it and stares me down again.

In front of everyone, I then ask why he only jumped twelve inches high when he and his coaches and teammates know he can jump thirty-eight inches high. Every time I have conducted this exercise in the National Football League, in the NCAA, or in a corporate business retreat, the player or employee has replied, "Because that is all you asked me to do."

This star player is one of the best athletes in the sport, and yet because of his contract, management often can't ask him to give more, do more, be more, or "jump higher." In business, we can't offer a raise every time we want someone to take his or her productivity to the next level. We can't motivate military or political leaders to increase their performance with money or recognition, either. We can motivate them to continue down the road toward significance only by expressing *expectations*—and not just any expectations, but expectations pegged to their own noble quest, their dream, their purpose.

What are your current expectations in the physical, mental, spiritual, emotional, social, financial, and familial sides of your life? How high is your bar compared to your potential? Who is stretching you? Because all the strengthening occurs in the area past the point of discomfort, and none of us can stretch ourselves to our ultimate capacity as human beings all by ourselves, we all need someone to raise our bar and, most important, to ask us to jump!

We also must dedicate ourselves to going above and beyond the right now—even if we're afraid or otherwise resistant. Obviously we can't jump higher than we are currently able, but still we must keep jumping. If you want to get better at doing push-ups, you get better and stronger by doing push-ups. It's easier to *act* our way into positive thinking than to think our way into positive action. Self-esteem, desire, and motivation are not required to change behavior. We need to change what we're doing—behavior changes behavior! When do most people fix their health problems? When it's too late. When do most people read a book on relationships? When their relationships are falling apart. We don't need to *feel* motivated to *do* motivated! It is not enough for us to *be* empathetic; we must *do* empathetic. It's not enough for our company to be customer-centric; we must *do* extraordinary customer service. We can't just *be* trustworthy, loyal, helpful, friendly, courteous, kind, obedient, cheerful, thrifty, brave, clean reverent, unconditionally loving, and forgiving; we must *do* them! It's not enough for us to *be* successful—we must *do* significance!

Becoming More of Who You Already Are

Because stretching entails a process of bringing change out from within, stretching implies a specific kind of competitive spirit. Successful individuals compete with others, measuring their success against what others accomplish. Significant individuals move along the growth path and attain both material and spiritual greatness by competing against themselves. Let me ask you: When you assess your own progress and growth, do you compare yourself to your neighbor down the street and the guy in the next cubicle? Or do you measure yourself against your dreams, your purpose, and the principles you yourself hold dear?

One person I know, love, and greatly admire who has stretched his entire life is the U.S. collegiate wrestling champion Anthony Robles. In 2011 Anthony won the National NCAA Wrestling Championship—with only one leg! I was privileged to write his acceptance speech as he received the ESPY Jimmy V Award for Perseverance on national television July 14, 2011. With the world watching, Robles humbly honored his mother for never giving up on him even though she, a teenaged single mother, could have thought that raising a child with one leg was too much and could have given up Anthony for adoption. When Anthony was in college and she herself became ill, and her husband walked out on the family, and they lost their home—she still didn't give up. His mother stretched to care for him and encouraged him to stretch to pursue his dreams of wrestling.

Robles recognized that not everyone understands the power of stretch: "At the beginning of my wrestling career, I lost most of my matches, and people said, 'It's okay. I'm proud of you for trying.' This ticked me off so bad! Losing is not okay! What they were really saying was that I was a handicapped kid and should be grateful that I could even participate." Following his mother, he refused to settle, stretched to achieve his goals, and has now dedicated his life to inspiring others to stretch. To express this dedication, he closed the speech with the following poem I wrote for the occasion:

Every soul who comes to earth

With a leg or two at birth

Must wrestle his opponents knowing

It's not what is, it's what can be, that measures worth.

Make it hard, just make it possible

And through pain. I'll not complain,

My spirit is unconquerable.

Fearless I will face each foe

For I know I am capable,

Making winning personal

I don't care what's probable

Through blood, sweat and tears,

I am Unstoppable!

Robles's story reveals that winning really is personal—and individual. While generic paths to success do exist—look at all the self-help books out there and the rules they expound—everybody's own path to significance is by definition an outgrowth of who they are and what they were intended to be on this planet. In measuring ourselves against ourselves, we should embrace our individuality and fearlessly verge into uncharted territory, even if others view us as quixotic or crazy.

To compete with oneself and to stretch from within brings us to the question: Do you first have to achieve success before you can achieve significance? The answer: a resounding Yes! A baby must drink before he eats, and only if he grows and strengthens can he learn to crawl before he walks and eventually runs. Every learning system is similar to studying mathematics, which begins with mastering the elementary, fundamental, preparatory laws of addition and subtraction, before we can comprehend and use the advanced laws of algebra and calculus. We need to learn how to do something perfectly, slowly, before we can learn to do it perfectly, quickly.

Stretching Others

After we have found our "physical therapist of the mind and heart" and have committed ourselves to stretching, we bear an immediate responsibility to reach out and start stretching others. To do so, we must recognize that a person can only grow from where he or she is.

To help others stretch, we must go to where they are physically and emotionally. I call this *mutual respect and support.*

An old high school teacher of mine, Mr. Croft, once mentioned to me that he had a student "who disrupted everything—a total terrorist."

"Did you kick him out and send him to the office?" I asked.

Mr. Croft shot me a mock-offended look. "I've taught school for over twenty-five years, and I've never sent a student to the principal's office. Most of my colleagues think the principal has all the Band-Aids. No way. Teachers are responsible for their classrooms and the development and education of each kid. I look at my classroom as my core of best customers, where I do eighty percent of my business with twenty percent of my clients. The classroom is like a sales territory, and I can't let any of my students leave or fail. I must sell them all something and then service the sale. You don't just throw them out when they do something wrong. We have to invite them to grow. We must catch them doing something right. You never know who will become your very best customer."

I shook my head and waved him off. "Mr. Croft, c'mon, this is Dan you're talking to. I've been to schools where a long line of students trails out the principal's office, down the hall, out the door, and past the bus stop. They're suntanned! And they just stand there with that look of, *Yep. I got caught screwing a goldfish into the pencil sharpener four months ago, and I'm on death row still waiting to see the principal.* So what did you do with your terrorist?"

Mr. Croft smiled. "Interesting you should ask. I didn't give up on him. I did my research and found that he played in a rock-and-roll band. One night, I went out to see him play in a smoke-filled, honky-tonk biker bar out in the bushes somewhere. I talked five teachers into going with me so I wouldn't be stabbed all by myself!"

Mr. Croft went on to relate that the whole room stopped when he and the other teachers entered, and the band stared them down. Visualize the wildest punk rockers who looked as though they had fallen down the stairs with a tackle box and been mugged by a staple gun! From the back of the room it looked as if the lead singer had a carburetor stuck in his nose, and the guitar player had twenty-two earrings in one ear and a miniature towel rack in the other ear. "When Johnny spotted us," Mr. Croft recounted, "he leaned into the microphone and yelled, 'What are you teachers doing here?'"

With cotton mouth and a fast-beating heart, Mr. Croft tried to be hip and yelled back, "We heard your band was groovy and we came to check you out." Laughing at the generation gap exposed by his choice of words, but feeling flattered and accepted, the band cranked back up their music. Mr. Croft and his fellow teachers stayed there for only fifteen minutes or so. "That's all the noise we could take!"

That was Friday night. On Monday morning, do you think Johnny was a discipline problem in Mr. Croft's class? No way! Was he a problem in Mr. Croft's class for the rest of the school year? No way! Was Johnny a discipline problem in other teachers' classrooms for the rest of the school year? Way! Was it because the others couldn't teach? No! It was simply because they expected their students to come to them. Mr. Croft made it his business to go where Johnny was—where he already felt comfortable. When it came to supporting Johnny as he stretched, it wasn't about Mr. Croft; it was about *Johnny*. Great teachers like Mr. Croft bend over backward to understand and deliver against their students' needs, desires, and perspectives—and to

show them that they care. Their students feel empowered, understanding that where they currently are is already the perfect place
from which to stretch and grow.

Stretching from the Ground Up

Stretch isn't limited to individuals. When employees at all levels of
the organizational hierarchy are inspired to stretch, they can take
entire companies with them. Among my thousands of clients, one of
my favorites is E-Z-GO, a division of Textron, the industrial con-
glomerate that includes Bell Helicopter, Cessna Aircraft Company,
and Greenlee, among others. Founded in 1954, E-Z-GO was a pio-
neer in the electric-vehicle field, becoming world renowned for its
golf cars. Yet by 2000 the golf cart business was stagnating, and
E-Z-GO had not introduced a major new product in almost a decade.
Even worse, the company's facilities and operating processes were
inefficient. The company had no established system for managing
inventory, scheduling production, or capturing and heeding the
voice of the customer.

Faced with the prospect of a slow, downward slide, E-Z-GO, newly
under CEO Kevin Holleran, took the usual steps turnaround companies take, revising business processes to realize efficiencies, improve
quality, and reduce costs. One crucial difference: Instead of prescribing
new policies from on high, Holleran drove transformation by encouraging individual employees to stretch themselves and jump higher.
Managers assessed the potential and current "height" of each employee's "broomstick bar," setting the bar at the level that would make the

company successful. They inspired employees to seize opportunities to stretch and provided tools (such as training in Six Sigma operational principles) to help them exceed past their own best personal performance and reach their full potential. E-Z-GO also kept employees informed about the company's goals in safety, quality, delivery, and cost, and linked individuals' own job-performance results to these metrics.

Once employees understood that they had the power to make a difference by stretching themselves, magic happened. Employee-driven projects and initiatives began spontaneously appearing all over the campus, ranging from new inventory-management systems to recycling programs to the use of solar tubes to harvest natural light and reduce energy costs. Kaizen events, which allowed entire, cross-functional teams of employees to brainstorm solutions and ideas for improvement, became commonplace.

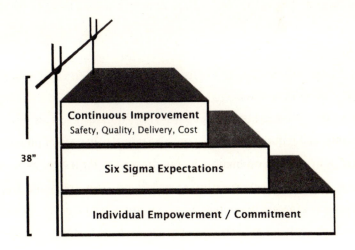

E-Z-GO's Ground-Up Stretch Formula

By 2008 E-Z-GO had substantially improved profitability and return on invested capital. In 2009 E-Z-GO received the Shingo Prize for Operational Excellence (often referred to as the "Nobel Prize" for manufacturing) and was named one of the top ten plants in North America by *IndustryWeek* magazine. In 2011 alone, E-Z-GO introduced more than a dozen new models. Today the company manufactures more than fifty vehicle models across three major brands and is growing rapidly into new markets. E-Z-GO is a classic example of why we must dedicate ourselves to stretching as high and as wide as we can at work, why leaders should create frameworks that support others to stretch, and what can happen if dedicated, passionate employees throughout an enterprise continually raise one another's broomsticks and stretch together in pursuit of an organizational goal.

The Bottom Line

Successful people obey the preparatory principle called change, altering what they do merely because others demand it of them. Significant individuals live the advanced, highest Law of Stretch, bringing personal transformation out from within, in a way that is meaningful to them. We stretch when we work hard to become everything we were meant to be in accordance with our own unique purpose and goals. It's a harder path but an immensely satisfying one. As I've seen firsthand, to stretch is to realize that what you learn, you learn by doing; that you walk firmer and more secure uphill than down. Successful people change their destinations and relish the arrival, while significant individuals stretch and thrive during the journey, willing at any moment to sacrifice what they are for who they could become. To stretch is to know that the greatest reward for your hard work is not what you get for it but what you become by it.

Four Suggested Action Steps to Learning to Stretch

1. Come to grips with the reality that no matter where you go, there you are; mere geographic relocation doesn't change much of anything. Now evaluate this "Balance Wheel" diagram combining nine aspects and areas of our lives:

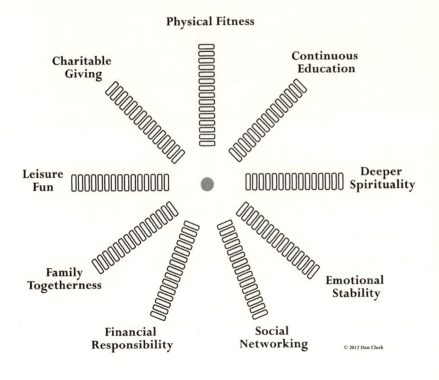

Physical Fitness

Charitable Giving

Continuous Education

Leisure Fun

Deeper Spirituality

Family Togetherness

Emotional Stability

Financial Responsibility

Social Networking

© 2012 Dan Clark

Rating yourself on a scale of 1 to 15 (15 being the highest level of performance), ponder how fully you've been living in the nine areas. Do you purposefully take care of your body? Do your keep your mind active? How fully have you been nurturing your soul with charitable deeds? Do you experience on a daily basis the vital emotions of fear, pain, joy, love, peace, and satisfaction? Do you approach your work with an eye toward always learning something new? Because no other success can compensate for failure in the home, and quantity time has a quality all its own, can your family see that they are the most important thing in the world to you?

Mark the boxes that reflect how you feel you are currently performing and draw a line to connect your number on the scale with each of the nine categories. This wheel is now a snapshot of your life. Which parts of your life are working best right now: body, mind, spirit, emotions, career, family and friends, or finances? Where can you improve—not all at once, but by one box, one day, one quality, one attribute, one task, at a time? Remember, when our lives get tough and our ride seems rough and bumpy, most blame the road, when in reality, it is ourselves we need to fix. Once we balance and round out our wheel, the ride is smooth and the way is rewarding.

2. Create your own personal "Board of Directors" made up of at least six people of all ages and professions, both men and women, representing three different religions (including your own). Because you absolutely love and respect these individuals, approach each with the humble request that he or she

becomes your "physical therapist" of the mind and heart—the person who will mentor you, helping you *stretch* from where you are to where you need to be.

3. With each of your mentors, make a list of only one thought and action in each of the nine areas that you can and will work on immediately. The objective: Stretch up just one notch number on the Balance Wheel measurement line. If you are at a level 7, the new and realistic goal will be to stretch to level 8. Step by step, line by line, precept upon precept, and stretch by stretch—you will become more of who you already are.

4. Each time you stretch and improve one number and one single step on the Balance Wheel scale, commit yourself in writing to sustaining this extraordinary thinking and fresh behavior until it becomes a new habit and personal pattern. This ensures that you'll never flip back to your previous mindsets and behaviors.

Trust Predictability Instead of Hope and Faith

Animals are reliable, many full of love, true in their affections, predictable in their actions, grateful and loyal. Difficult standards for people to live up to.

—ALFRED MONTAPER

As should be apparent by now, the higher path I'm calling significance involves the assumption of risk. It is risky to commit ourselves to obeying higher laws and to persevering day after day. Stretching also involves willingly stepping into risk for the sake of discovering more of who we already are. So, what drives and fortifies us to take risks? Some combination of hope and faith that obedience to a law will bear fruit; hope that our efforts will help us achieve our goals motivates all that we do, from getting dressed in the morning to watering the lawn to going to work. We wouldn't bother planting a seed if we didn't have hope or faith that it would grow, nor would we take time to learn anything if we didn't have hope or faith that our undertaking would benefit us. Hope and faith propel us to give anything a try.

From another perspective, however, hope and faith are relatively empty concepts. Spiritual guides teach us that faith is not to have a perfect knowledge of things; if we have faith we hope for things which are not seen, which are true. But too many people live their lives hoping to be happy, and because they only hope, they never really are. Too many religionists drop to their knees to pray and pray, forgetting to stand on their feet and do their part in facilitating an answer to that prayer. Hope and faith amount to mere optimism and a positive outlook, without anything substantive to back them up.

Trust, by contrast, is a form of optimism that's actually grounded in something—a deep and abiding knowledge of the people we're trusting. No, our knowledge isn't perfect, and we sometimes wind up with our trust betrayed. But when we trust, whether in ourselves or others, it is because we have become aware, over time, of who we are and because we can take assurance in the predictability and consistency of *us*. Unlike hope and faith, trust is *earned*—it means something. Hope and faith allow us to speculate on the possibilities; trust founded on real knowledge allows us to *calculate the probabilities*. Hope is blind and oftentimes a reckless risk; trust is a *calculated* risk. To walk the path of significance, we must transcend mere hope and faith and embrace *trust*—in ourselves, in our colleagues, in our relationships, in our world. One of my mentors, Dick Grace, celebrates the advanced, highest Law of Trust by observing, "To risk is to momentarily lose your footing. Not to risk is to permanently lose your self. To regain your footing and balance, trust yourself."

Getting Real with Ourselves

Trusting begins with unconditional love and nonjudgmental acceptance, which is how we put faith and hope into action. Learning to
trust ourselves means becoming brutally honest in acknowledging
who we are, even the parts of ourselves we might not like. We must
know and accept the absolute truth regarding our origin, place, and
relationship with the universe, staring our failures and shortcomings
in the face. And we must dispense with many of the common myths
we fall back on to hide and explain away our shortcomings when the
going gets tough.

Chief among these myths are what psychologists call the Four
Myths of Feeling: "I can make you feel good; I can make you feel
bad; you can make me feel good; you can make me feel bad." No.
Nobody can *make* us feel any way other than the way we *choose* to
feel. *The only thing we are not in charge of is whether or not we are in
charge.* We have the power to feel unless we decide to relinquish this
power to someone else. And when we don't feel happy or satisfied,
we need to reflect on what *we* are doing to make ourselves feel as we
do. We need to understand and accept our own tendencies in the act
of taking responsibility for them.

If you're angry at your boss, ask yourself: What have *you* done to
become angry? Why are *you* letting your boss's actions get to you?
What are your patterns and trigger points? If your boss is angry at
you, what is *he* doing to himself in the moment to bring about that
emotion? And shouldn't you stop playing the role of the pleaser,
thinking you need to mollify your boss at every turn, when, in
fact, he needs to accept responsibility for his own feelings?

When we relinquish our power, our helplessness tends to escalate, incorporating still other excuses that obscure self-understanding. We all, I'm sure, will recognize elements of what I call the Five Theories of Action:

- *The "It's Not My Job" Theory*, where you refuse to exceed expectations or do anything beyond the call of duty. You don't come early or stay late unless it is written in your contract or you receive overtime pay.
- *The "Gene" Theory*, where it's hereditary. You can't do anything about your constitutional, genetic makeup. You're stuck with a negative personality, bad temper, slow motor skills, and lack of imagination simply because your father's personality is negative. Or you get it from your mother.
- *The "Cosmic" Theory*, where the universe and the world are the way they are, and you can't do anything about it.
- *The "Astrology" Theory*, where you were born under a specific sign of the zodiac, on a certain date with specific planets and moons lined up. This accounts for your assigned personality, and the stars will control your destiny.

And finally . . .

- *The "Meant to Be" Theory*, which means you have no free will, choice, or agency to affect the outcome of your life and destiny. You are merely a pawn in our Creator's chess game. Meant-to-be suggests that Princess Diana's death in an automobile accident with a drunken chauffer was meant to be; John F. Kennedy Jr. and his wife and sister-in-law died in a plane crash because his lack of flight training was meant to be; two teenagers attempt suicide—one lives, one dies—because it was meant to be. Why build hospitals or call for an ambulance? It doesn't matter what we do. The situation, circumstances, and outcome are meant to be.

My response to all of this is: Are you *serious*? Some people actually believe that a Creator or Supreme Being orchestrated two hundred people from thirty-five different states and five foreign countries to board TWA flight 800 from New York to Paris on the same day. And when the plane blows up and kills everybody—it was meant to be? And when a businesswoman got in an argument with her husband that day, which caused her to miss this flight, these unkind words were also meant to be?

Drivers can drink, pilots can err, planes can malfunction, air traffic controllers can screw up, teenagers can get confused, the female reproductive system can be traumatized or an abnormal chromosome can produce birth defects, we can all get sick, earthquakes can cause tsunamis and devastation in Thailand, Haiti, Chile, and Japan, but none of these circumstances or events were caused by divine intervention or orchestrated by a mystical influence. If these calamities and tragedies were meant to be, it is because the universe was organized by a set of laws, and when any one of the laws is not obeyed or collides with another corresponding or noncorresponding law, some unexpected bad things can happen to good people.

The 2004 Indian Ocean earthquake, officially called the Sumatra–Andaman earthquake, was an undersea megathrust quake caused by subduction, the sideways and downward movement of the edge of a plate of the earth's crust into the mantle beneath another plate. With a magnitude of 9.3, this was the third largest quake ever recorded, and the one with the longest duration. It caused the entire planet to vibrate as much as one centimeter, triggering other earthquakes as far away as Alaska, inundating coastal communities with waves up to ninety-eight feet high, and killing over 230,000 people in fourteen countries. The tsunami wasn't "meant to be"; it occurred, ultimately, because of the basic laws of physics governing the movement of tectonic plates and oceans.

We humans believe in the Four Myths of Feeling and the Five Theories of Action for one reason: We're afraid. These excuses serve to eliminate the stress that comes with taking responsibility for our lives and dealing with tragedy, disappointment, discouragement, real depression, and failure. Yet stress elimination comes at a cost. The more we fall back on excuses, the less we actually know ourselves in all our ambiguity and complexity, and the less able we are to trust ourselves. When we're afraid of others, we can't meet them with trust, either; and when we're afraid of life, there's nothing left to trust.

Everybody's Born with a Conscience

Now, you might ask: If we peel away the layers of subterfuge and really confront ourselves, will what we find inspire our trust? Yes, and I'll tell you why: Trust is based one hundred percent on predictability, and predictability is always linked to consistency. As we learned in Law 1, "The Law of Obedience," every person on this planet carries an innate sense of right and wrong, a natural ability to decipher between good and evil. Conscience, as we call this gut instinct, is that little voice in our heads that whispers, "Do unto others as you would have them do unto you; do the right thing simply because it's the right thing to do." Conscience is the reason we experience a natural attraction to ethical codes of conduct and instinctively live by moral-based core values, both in business and in life.

We can feel secure that our conscience will never fail us. True, our desire to follow our conscience can waver; it decreases as we continue to do the wrong thing, because error desensitizes our awareness and quarantines us in a place past the point of feeling. It's like walking into a room that stinks so bad you want to retch, but if you stay there long enough, you become accustomed to the smell, and it doesn't bother you anymore. Still, our conscience itself remains true. As far as we may stray, we can always reconnect to it if and when we're willing to do the work.

As evidence of our intrinsic ability to know what is good and bad, right and wrong, and our ability to truthfully judge when and if we decide to, we need only speak with teenagers, and ask them one question, "If you had you for a child, would you be nervous?" Most cringe and laugh, "Whoa, I wouldn't even let me go out! I would have grounded myself as a baby!" Voilà! A kid's conscience exposed and constantly at work for all to see.

Because we all possess consciences, we can take comfort in the notion that life's most important answers already lie inside of each of us. We can affirm that there are no mistakes in life, only lessons, and that a lesson is repeated, sometimes presented in various forms, until we learn it. If we don't learn easy lessons, they get harder. Life has no meaning except the meaning we give it—precisely why it's important to associate with the appropriate conscience-following individuals whom you can trust to help you figure it all out.

Trust Others as if Life Depends on It—Because It Does!

That brings me to relationships. Trust is the most important ingredient in every relationship. It's the most difficult leadership and friendship element to develop, the easiest to lose, and clearly the toughest to ever regain. Trust is also the critical first step to building a winning team and launching and sustaining a profitable business. Without trust, every relationship is shallow and fleeting. Because we are interdependent as human beings living in a global society, trust is our most important connector.

Just as our ability to trust ourselves originates in a perception of consistency and predictability, so, too, does our ability to trust other people. You can trust people who are so consistent that you can actually predict what they will think and do and how they will react in every situation. We trust our spouses and significant others to be in mixed company out of our presence and feel no jealousy because we know exactly how our trusted one has behaved in the past. We trust coworkers because they keep their promises by getting to work on time, sticking to their ten-minute breaks and forty-five-minute lunches, coming in early and staying late to help the team get the job done on time. When fellow employees and teammates are consistently honest, loyal, and helpful, they are predictably positive, productive, and worthy of our full, unconditional trust.

In no other work environment have I encountered such constant and intense trust than in the U.S. Military, especially the U.S. Air Force. As pilots from all aircrafts have repeatedly told me, "We meticulously fly by trust in teamwork. Teamwork begins and ends with cooperation and coordination, which can only come through complete and total trust."

Formation flying constitutes an especially startling display of trust in motion. In my ride in a T-38 jet trainer at Randolph Air Force Base in San Antonio, Texas, we took off in formation with another aircraft and flew in formation for sixty minutes in acrobatic air show maneuvers only three feet apart from wing to wing. When we landed, flight instructor Lieutenant Colonel Ben Stagg explained to me that formation flying is done entirely by sight, called triangulation. You keep your eyes fixed on the lead airplane next to you, forming a triangle between the wing tip, the thickness of the wing, and the stub aileron at the back of the tail. The goal is to keep the triangle always the same in relation to the distance and position of your aircraft to the other. The pilot in the lead plane determines everything you do and everywhere you go. Altitude, speed, direction—you do not question; you only follow.

How do formation pilots do it? Do they rely on hope or faith? No. Faith without works is not faith at all. Stagg was clear that it is not blind faith. You don't follow the lead pilot because you are blind, but because you see. You see in his abilities hard work, integrity, and excellence. Therefore, flying in formation is about trust. You are holding your control stick, and the other pilot is holding his. Because of preparation and perfect practice, you trust your *feel* for the control stick. You trust *your* eye-hand coordination, and out of trust and respect for the other pilot's commitment to excellence and preparation, you have trust in his *feel* for flying.

Trustworthy Institutions

Trustworthy individuals give rise to trustworthy institutions. The world-famous Mayo Clinic in Rochester, Minnesota, has won the trust of my entire family, and I'd like to tell you why.

In 1984 my dad was diagnosed with malignant carcinoid cancer in his stomach, intestines, and liver, and given only six months to live. He didn't have the strength to walk and was confined to a wheelchair.

A week later, Dad qualified as one of twenty-five patients to participate in an exclusive experimental treatment program at the Mayo Clinic. From the minute we arrived, Mayo extraordinarily distinguished itself from all other hospitals: There was no wait at admissions, and my dad was made to feel as though he was the single most important person who ever walked through their doors. The nurses carefully wheeled my dad into a large room where we met "Team Mayo," headed up by world-renowned oncologist Dr. Allan Schutt. The motivational moment for me was when my dad was asked, "Is there a difference between dying of cancer and living with cancer, and what would it be for you?"

Seven days later, my dad walked out of the Mayo Clinic on his own, with renewed physical and emotional strength, stable vital signs, and a real belief that they were all going to help him fight off his horrible disease if he himself would lead the fight.

On a subsequent visit back to Mayo, this time alone, my dad experienced what my family calls the "Mayo Way." Doctors were going to test him using a special echocardiograph. A tube is inserted into the patient's esophagus so that the operator can more closely examine the heart than a traditional cardiograph would permit. The echocardiograph machine was new, and other American hospitals had not yet acquired it. In due course, Dad lay on the table with the incredible Dr. A. Jamil Tajik and a nurse hovering over him. Here's what my dad wrote in his journal:

After preparations got under way, including the spraying of my throat to make it numb and more receptive to the black tube, Dr. Tajik asked me if I had any of my family with me. I told him that I was alone. He said there were some risks in using the machine that he had to advise me of. At the end of the tube was a mirror-like tip through which the action of the heart was relayed to a screen. The good doctor explained that as he attempted to thrust the tube down my throat he might cut the esophagus, or he might even cut the heart. I asked him, "What then?" and he replied that I could die on the table. With a deep breath, I knew I could trust a Mayo doctor and agreed to the procedure. The first try the tube would not go down. He pulled it back up, and the second time he was successful.

Dad concluded:

I presume that the nurse noticed a tear in my eye that dropped and ran down my cheek as we proceeded with the test. She promptly and gently held my hand and began to whisper and assure me that everything would be all right. I had never felt the need for third-party support as strongly as I did at that moment. And in the "Mayo Way," that dear nurse, whose name I will probably never know, gave me, through her soft, confident voice and compassionate, tender touch, a beautiful fulfillment that I should trust the doctor, trust her that all would be fine. As I lay helpless on that uncomfortable bed a thousand miles from home, she refused to let me feel alone.

Because of the Mayo Clinic's polished professionalism and compassionate service, we were able to enjoy and continue to learn from my dad for another six and a half years. Every twelve weeks, my dad excitedly traveled cross-country to Mayo for seven days of tests and treatments. He said he fought hard to live because he wanted to give all he could to Mayo and help them advance their specialized treatment for carcinoid cancer. Because of my dad's successful, long-term care, the FDA approved the drug given to him for regular use in other U.S. hospitals.

My dad loved the Mayo Clinic, and so do all of us in the Clark clan. We have faith in the Mayo Clinic, and we hope for the best for all their patients, but even more than that, we trust them. The consistent kindness and hard work of the doctors and nurses there has earned that trust. We need more organizations like the Mayo Clinic. What can your organization do starting today to provide services that earn similar levels of trust?

The Bottom Line

Successful people subscribe to the preparatory principles of hope and faith. Significant individuals live the advanced, highest Law of

Trust. Hope and faith amount to blind, easy optimism, whereas trust is grounded in past experience and actually *means* something. We trust others (and ourselves) because we have taken time to know them and examine them honestly, thus certifying them as worthy of our trust. As significant people understand, trust is given, received, and fully accepted only when it is earned, when all parties involved do what they should, when they should, giving it everything they've got when less would be sufficient, not because others expect superior effort, but because they demand it of themselves—because their consciences demand it. Trust is the backbone and conscience is the spinal cord of every meaningful relationship, even relationships we have with institutions. Without trust and conscience, relationships die.

Four Suggested Action Steps to Learning to Trust

1. Make a list of five people you trust and determine why you trust them. Commit to emulate their character traits, attributes, and qualities.

2. Look for, solicit, and secure an opportunity to showcase your leadership skills so people can see that you are responsible, accountable, dependable, and trustworthy. By the same token, help others establish themselves as trustworthy. Let your eleven-year-olds baby-sit and mow lawns, your thirteen-year-olds travel with their sports teams on overnight trips, your sixteen-year-olds learn to drive, and your eighteen-year-olds vote for the candidate of his or her informed choice. How else,

Aristotle would ask, do we expect our kids to learn to be trustworthy except by letting them do trustworthy acts?

3. Practice thinking before you talk. Take time to write down what you know and believe about certain issues before you are asked to share your views. Then focus on saying what you mean, meaning what you say, being consistent by always following through on every one of your responses, and always doing what you say you are going to do.

4. Do something that will frighten you and push you beyond your comfort zone: a trapeze course, bungee jumping, a super zip-line, sky diving. Because each of these high-adventure activities requires that you have a worker strap you into a harness, you will experience what it means to totally trust both a person and a thing. When the adrenaline leaves your body, you will comprehend fully that trust is built through predictability and by that count superior to hope and faith.

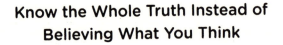

Law 5

Know the Whole Truth Instead of Believing What You Think

Cities, like San Francisco, are literary art. Every block is a short story, every hill a novel, every home a poem, every dweller within immortal. That is the whole truth.

—WILLIAM SAROYAN

We've seen that trust originates in knowledge, yet there's a wrinkle: Not all knowledge is created equal. Some contentions are true whether or not we believe them—and whether or not we like them—whereas other contentions amount to mere untested belief. We can trust on the basis of mere belief, but what if our belief fails us and we trust the wrong people and incorrect principles? What if you lived your life trusting your computer spell check to get your critical documents accurate, instead of doing your own proofreading? Have you ever typed something like "Do not expect spell check to catch all your mistakes," and your computer displayed "Donut except spillceck too cache all you're miss steaks," and you didn't check it because you believed everything was going to turn out perfectly?

Successful people satisfy themselves with trusting on the basis of untested beliefs, many of which turn out correct, partially correct, or absolutely incorrect. Significant people go further and do the work of constantly testing and broadening their beliefs to arrive at the *whole truth*. They feel secure and comfortable in their trust because it rests on deep, full, hard-won knowledge.

From the limited perspective of those who don't understand the difference between success and significance, who look at the world only through the lens of their mental conditioning, personal ignorance, and limited experience, life can seem depressing, chaotic, unfair, and meaningless. I compare this perspective with people walking into the middle of a three-act play. Those without the whole truth do not understand what happened in the first act and the purposes established there; nor do they understand the clarification and resolution that come in the third act, which makes worthwhile all the sacrifice and hard work required in the second act. Without the whole and complete truth, we can never appreciate the comprehensive plan required to take ourselves from hello to goodbye—from where we are to where we want to be. Consequently, we feel disadvantaged and penalized.

The nineteenth-century minister Henry Ward Beecher exhorted: "Hold yourself responsible for a higher standard than anybody else expects of you. Never excuse yourself. Never pity yourself. Be a hard master to yourself—and be lenient to everybody else." Significant people are the hardest of masters when it comes to knowledge. They conduct an ongoing and endless audit of their own beliefs. If and when these beliefs don't hold water, significant people adjust, broaden, and deepen their thinking. The path to significance is thus profoundly intellectual—a constant expansion in our perception of the world, a constant strengthening of mind.

Beware the Weak Mind

No matter where we are in our mental, emotional, and spiritual development, we can always work to become more significant by controlling and strengthening our minds. Unfortunately, so many of us shrink before the challenge. We either fear thinking or don't know how. We think with our hopes or wishes rather than with our minds. We think when in fact we are only rearranging our prejudices. Even if we bother to explore new theories and entertain other opinions, we may wind up holding several opinions about the same thing every week, leaving our original beliefs intact amid all the confusion. And so we remain far indeed from perceiving the whole truth.

What are some of your most cherished beliefs? Do you regularly submit them to scrutiny, or do you push inconvenient evidence or arguments out of your mind? (We'll explore more on this topic below.) Do you ask subordinates at work to tell you what you need to know, or do you give signals that they should tell you only what you want to hear? How far do you really go to find the whole truth?

As the philosopher William George Jordan reminds us, "The man who has a certain religious belief and fears to discuss it, lest it may be proved wrong, is not loyal to his beliefs, he has but a coward's faithfulness to his prejudices. If he were a lover of truth, he would be willing at any moment to surrender his belief for a higher, better, and truer faith."

Sometimes the most successful, strong-willed people possess surprisingly weak minds, valuing their entrenched beliefs more than the cause of truth itself. Sometimes we cling to beliefs because we worry that not doing so will threaten our continued success. Weak minds worry, which affects the circulation, the heart, the glands, the nervous system—our entire health. Many have died from worry and doubt. Three fourths of the mistakes we make occur because we do not really know what we think we know. Consequently, we doubt our abilities, our purpose, and our worthiness to proceed. We grow unhappy.

Thirty days after the terrible events of 9/11, elementary school administrators and teachers across America noticed that young children came to school in a state of panic. In response to a nationwide survey asking them what had happened on that day, children offered the same response: Bad men stole jets and crashed them into buildings, killing thousands of people, and they kept doing it. Adult leaders and we parents failed to realize that our impressionable and vulnerable children couldn't distinguish between the continual video replays on the news and real-time reality. Watching television, kids saw repeated footage and actually thought we had been attacked eight to ten times a day for thirty days in a row. Their response reveals a complicated reality that applies to adults as well: We are tormented by our *ideas* of things, not by the things themselves. The weaker, less tested, and narrower our minds are, the more susceptible to torment we become.

Overcoming Fear

Fear is real: Fear of the unknown; fear of the economy's worsening; fear of losing a job, a house, or good health; fear of falling; fear of speaking in public; fear of dying. All fears drain our energy, stifle our creativity, destroy our concentration, and immobilize our self-image. Regardless of whether there is truly something to fear, we must deal with all fears in the same way: By learning the whole truth. We cannot succeed or become significant in ignorance. Strength of mind renders us happier and more whole, precisely because it eliminates doubt and inspires confidence. History's greatest teachers have all affirmed that if we are prepared, we will not fear—that the only thing we have to fear is fear itself. And the way to prepare is to inform ourselves about the total picture.

In sales, fear, anxiety, and the so-called quota pressure go away when we implicitly know our value proposition; have an in-depth, comprehensive product knowledge; and know the right answers and correct techniques to overcome the toughest objections before the sales presentation begins. In sports, the fear of our opponent, the anxiety of competing, or the sudden lack of confidence, fueled by a fear of losing, all vanish when we learn the whole truth about our opponents or the competition. When we implicitly know our playbook and assignments, and when we have studied and memorized the strengths, weaknesses, situational tendencies, offensive strategies, defensive schemes, and favorite plays of our competitor, we learn the whole truth and become fearless.

Think again about your own fears: Is there a side of the picture you have not considered? When you're afraid of something, do you tend to avoid it, or do you push against your emotions and learn more about the source of your fear? Is there a way that you can back away, climb to higher ground, and apprehend the total size, depth, breadth, and magnitude of the landscape?

Truths and Whole Truths

Overcoming fear by getting to the whole truth isn't easy; it requires discipline and close scrutiny to carefully separate truths from virtues, values, principles, and the details used to explain them. Side-by-side comparison of a few half-truths and whole truths will suggest the substantial gap between truth and whole truth, and the kind of thought and active study required to bridge that gap.

As we can all agree, the truth about wealth is that it comes by knowing how to make money. The *whole truth* is that wealth flows through you, not to you; you can get anything in life you want if you are willing to help enough other people get what they want.

The truth is we can hear. The *whole truth* is that we should listen.

The truth is there are problems. The *whole truth* is they are challenges.

The truth is the glass is either half empty or half full. The *whole truth* is that it could be half full of the wrong thing.

The truth is that if you are overweight and see yourself in the mirror as a fat failure, you are staying negative and not motivating change. The *whole truth* is that if you see yourself as someone who has been very successful at putting on weight, you will realize that you gained it one pound at a time and therefore can lose it one pound at a time.

The truth is that you should find a good-paying job. The *whole truth* is that you should find your life's work and what you feel your calling is.

The truth in finance is that assets and liabilities listed on a balance sheet determine a company's market value. The *whole truth* is that the most valuable parts of companies are brought there by employees.

The truth is that pain hurts. The whole truth is that pain is a signal to grow, not just to suffer.

The truth is that a crisis causes stress. The whole truth is that a crisis does not make or break the person—it just reveals the character within.

The whole truth about life is that some things are true whether we believe them or not—everybody is entitled to their own opinions, but nobody is entitled to the wrong facts—truth is truth wherever it's found.

We can sum up by saying that truth is untested belief; *whole truth* is hard-won wisdom. And hard-won wisdom is precisely what frees us from our fears.

Freedom of the Press?

Earlier I noted that many of us shrink from the challenge of pursuing whole truth. I'd like to pick up that theme by highlighting a trap we often fall into in our public life, a phenomenon social scientists call confirmation bias. Under confirmation bias, decision makers seek out and assign more weight to evidence confirming their hypotheses and ignore or don't fully consider evidence negating their hypotheses.

In public discussions, confirmation bias plagues us by saddling us with self-fulfilling social, political, and racial prejudices. Investigators and journalists often perpetuate confirmation bias by framing data in ways that confirm their views and personal conclusions, as in the case of the many theories on the assassination of President John F. Kennedy that to this day still stir controversy. Or television news programs where the producer chooses "expert guests" based on whether the guest shares the producer's political and social biases. Is this not a mockery of our sacred and cherished freedom of the press?

In 2005 I had a chance to see confirmation bias at work during my first visit to Iraq. After delivering a speech in the grand ballroom of one of Saddam Hussein's palaces in Baghdad, I met with the officials who two weeks earlier had conducted Iraq's first-ever free election. These leaders had set up the polling stations, delivered the voting ballots, and retrieved them for counting. I saw the map of locations and heard incredible election-day stories. In Iraq, a country the size of California, there were 5,578 polling stations and only eleven explosions. Yet all we heard about in the States were the eleven explosions! Why? Because those eleven explosions—but not the larger context of the 5,578 polling stations—confirmed the bias of journalists who had already believed that our Iraq policy had failed.

Upon arriving back home, I went on some national TV programs to talk about my experiences. When I shared my story about the blatant confirmation bias involved in the reporting, the journalist became indignant. "Are you saying there is no integrity in our news networks?"

"No!" I replied. "We trust you and know that there is a regulatory checks-and-balances system in place. What I'm saying is that the news media often gives us the right answers to the wrong questions." I went on to remind this journalist that he or she who asks the questions controls the conversation. You can get right, correct, truthful, *negative* answers if you ask negative questions, and go down a negative path; and you can get right, correct, truthful, *positive* answers if you ask positive questions and go down a positive path. By asking only certain kinds of questions, we allow ourselves to ignore inconvenient facts or accept mere speculation as fact. Such tendentious questioning can yield information that proves just about anything to our own satisfaction and enables us to get what we want. However, by failing to grasp the whole truth, we won't want what we get—and on that count, we'll stray far from the higher path of significance.

Significant journalists make conscious efforts to avoid confirmation bias. So, too, does our justice system. When I was called for jury duty, lawyers assembled all forty potential jurors and explained that we were being considered to hear a case. But before we could do so, they had to weed out any biases we might have had. The case involved an illegal immigrant who, allegedly while driving drunk and without a license, hit a car and killed a child in the backseat. The defense attorney asked if we knew anyone who had ever been hit by a drunk driver and if we thought illegal immigrants should be allowed to stay in the country. Any juror who answered yes to the first question and no to the second was dismissed. These questions helped prevent jurors from allowing their biases to affect the verdict. If a potential juror responded emotionally to drunk driving because of a traumatic incident, or if he or she already harbored resentment toward illegal immigrants, then emotion could prevent that juror from fairly considering all the evidence in this particular case and delivering a fair ruling.

Unfortunately, awareness of bias does not pervade all areas of our justice system—not by a long shot! When U.S. Supreme Court Justice William Rehnquist died of cancer in 2005 and shortly thereafter Justice Sandra Day O'Connor announced her retirement, no one paid much attention to the qualifications of the future justices. Countless attorneys and judges made the short list of possible appointees based on the prestige of their law school, their ranking in their graduating class, the number of cases they tried and won, and their years of experience practicing law. But the nomination and confirmation process by the Senate is not about best; it is only about the Left and the Right.

Feedback: The Breakfast of Champions

If the wrong questions lead to confirmation bias, which leads us away from whole truth, continual, real-time, up-to-the-minute feedback brings us that much closer. Feedback is the breakfast of champions, telling us more of the truth so we can adjust our actions. When NASA launched a rocket to the moon, feedback determined its direction and destination. When the rocket went off course, astronauts heard beeps and either electronically or manually corrected the course. Question: What would happen if NASA launched the rocket and waited ninety days to check up on it, as some do in the corporate world with their quarterly reports? We all know that the quicker we recognize weakness, mediocrity, misdirection, or failure, the easier and more cost effective it is to fix it, change it, and get ourselves back on track toward our desired destination. We stand accountable not only for what we do, but also for what we *don't* do. And what matters is not only what we know, but what we *don't* know.

Compare two winter Olympic events that often take place on the same ice rink—figure skating and ice hockey. During the Olympic Winter Games in Salt Lake City in 2002, I attended the pairs figure skating finals. Two skaters emerged from backstage, smiling and holding hands, as their names came over the PA system and skated to their places in the center of the ice. They adopted a John Travolta–esque, one-arm-up *Saturday Night Fever* disco pose. The music began and off they went. After spinning each other around a few times, triple axel–ing it up, and one-legging it down, they ended their routine four minutes later.

The audience gave an appreciative, polite, sophisticated applause, but then waited in dead silence.

"How did they do?" I asked the stranger sitting next to me.

"Don't know yet," she said.

"Why?"

"The scorers' table hasn't flashed the judges' scores yet," the woman explained.

I was baffled. Everyone had watched a routine for four minutes, and we didn't even know what we just saw! (How many of us sit at our desks at the end of a workday with the same shocked, puzzled, deer-in-the-headlights look, wondering what happened?)

As two more minutes of waiting passed, images of the two skaters sitting in the kiss-and-cry area flashed up on the arena's Jumbotron. They held hands, out of breath and sweating, while a sportscaster interviewed them with classy questions like, "So, did you fall on purpose?" Then the arena erupted as the scorers' table finally flashed the judges' scores: 4.5, 4.5, 4.6, 1.2 (from the Russian judge!), and 8.6 (from the French judge, who forgot that there was a 6-point maximum!). Tears flowed; the skaters were devastated.

What a tragedy, I thought. *All those thousands of hours, all those years of training, for this letdown. Their dreams of world championships and Olympic gold had slipped away.* The scorekeeping system had no way to adapt or adjust during the performance. Although most professional skaters can intuit for themselves roughly how they are doing in the moment, the all-important formal feedback measurement came at the end of the task, when it was too late to change anything. I pulled out my pad and jotted down my observation: *"Increasing our frequency of feedback allows us to change our behavior before it is too late!"*

The next day, I attended the gold medal ice hockey game. What a difference! In figure skating, the fans sit quietly with their arms to their sides. They wear sport coats and ties, dresses, and pantsuits in a sophisticated, reverent, elegant-based environment of class. Hockey fans bring their own pucks so they can throw them at each other. The fans drink and then spill more than they drink. At the slightest sneer, smirk, or cheap shot, the players drop their gloves to rearrange one another's faces. A lawsuit was recently filed in New York because two fans climbed over the glass and beat up the opposing team's coach. Clearly, ice hockey is the number one cause of prison riots in North America. When inmates watch hockey on TV they become uncontrollably mad when they see a hockey player get a five-minute penalty for the exact same offense they are doing seventeen years for!

While figure skating has no feedback, in hockey, everybody—the fans, the coaches, and especially the players—can see the scoreboard and know at all times the score and the time remaining. If his team is losing by a goal with a minute left, the coach doesn't quit and say, "I can't take it, we lost, buy me a hot dog." Instead, he adjusts, takes out the goalkeeper, and puts in a sixth attacker to tie up the game and send it into overtime.

In business management, we can't afford to wait until the quarterly report comes out in April to learn how we did in January and February. In sales, we can't afford to wait until the end of the month to learn how our totals-versus-quota ratios tallied. In family life, parents can't wait until a child is eighteen to keep him or her off drugs and offer feedback that teaches their child about sexuality and moral responsibility. We need *whole truth*—as best as we can apprehend it— at all times. Why is it so difficult for so many to understand that it's better to build a fence at the edge of a cliff than to park an ambulance at its base? It's better to prepare and prevent than to repent and repair! We must stop and ask ourselves both professionally and personally: Is my system of measurement feedback more like figure skating or ice hockey? Do I know what's going on at all times—the whole truth—so I can quickly make essential choices along the way? Or is change, positive and especially negative, always a surprise?

Three Forms of Feedback

As we strive to increase our frequency of feedback, it helps to distinguish the following three forms of feedback.

Factual feedback constitutes the cold, hard facts of our current reality, data to which we assign accountability without blame. A person's performance does not improve or increase with blame; that serves only to make the person feel worse. Factual feedback, by contrast, is neither positive nor negative—it just is. It tells us what the score is, how far for a first down, and what yard line the ball is on—information that allows us to measure the progress toward reaching the goal. In the 1994 Winter Olympics, Alberto Tomba, the top-ranked ski racer in the world, finished in an embarrassing twelfth place after the first slalom run. But because of factual feedback, he knew exactly what he needed to do down to the 100th of a second, and he went all out in his second and final Olympic run. With pride and reckless abandon, Tomba skied like a madman until he crossed the finish line, this time way ahead of the entire field, until he was beaten by .10 second by the final racer. Tomba won silver.

Motivational feedback is the cheering crowd and encouraging coach who tells us, "You can do it—go for it!" We need motivational feedback to get us to hustle; it triggers the adrenaline and endorphins we need to dig deep and compete. As a professional speaker, I have realized that most convention attendees want less information and more motivation and acknowledgment that they are performing well. Motivational feedback must not only celebrate excellence and winning; it must also celebrate improvement, which stimulates more improvement.

Educational feedback is correctional coaching—such as that that changed and improved Tomba's ski run, or betters our job performance at work. It's the teacher telling the child, "I love the way you attempt this math problem, but this is the change you must understand and implement to get the correct and desired answer."

If our goal is significance, no one of these forms of feedback will suffice, because no single form on its own will yield the whole truth.

By increasing how often we receive all three forms of feedback, we are not only able to change our behavior, but we also can pick the most appropriate behavior to positively effect the outcome of a task, event, or game. Feedback in all its forms confronts us with the clear choices we face, and then it's up to us to make the right decision.

Making the right decision, at the right time, for the right reason is always predicated on receiving whole truth through timely feedback. I witnessed this during a college basketball game where the teams had gone back and forth, changing leads the entire evening. When only three seconds remained in the game, one team was behind by one point and called a final time-out. Then the whistle blew and play resumed. A player on the team behind by one threw the ball in bounds. A second teammate caught the ball, turned, and shot. The ball was airborne when the buzzer sounded. The game ended as the ball ripped through the net for the win. The team down by one had won by two! Why? How? Pandemonium erupted.

When the player caught the inbounds pass, he didn't turn, sprint up the court, and take a short jump shot. He turned and threw the ball like a baseball the whole length of the court to the other basket— ninety feet away! Talk about a three-pointer! That's not a real high-percentage shot! Question: What would the coach have said to that player had he taken that shot in the middle of the first quarter? Most likely, "Calm down! Why don't you bounce it a couple more times before you launch another one?"

But because of his exposure to up-to-the-minute correct information, the player was able to alter his actions and behaviors and match them to the specific needs required at that specific moment to be successful in that specific circumstance. The player had access to all three forms of feedback that together yielded whole truth: He knew the score and time remaining (factual), was encouraged by the fans and his fellow teammates (motivational), and likely heard a word or two of advice from his coach (educational). As an aside, this hero player who made the game-winning basket had missed his previous nine shots. Apparently the coach had emphasized the positive and reinforced his belief and confidence in this player throughout the entire game, especially when the team was behind, which allowed the player to rise to the occasion when it mattered the most.

Learning from Disneyland

Continuously high levels of feedback enable superior, in-the-moment performance in the business world, too. I once went to Disneyland with my family. As we entered the long line to go on Space Mountain, a Disney employee handed me a time card. When I was still in line an hour later, another employee took the card and documented how long I had been holding it. I trust that this information about my wait was evaluated and acted upon, because the next day, with more people at the park, I went on the same ride at the exact same time of day, and I had to wait only twenty-seven minutes. It turns out that through their intense and constant measurement-feedback system, Disney can tell that people wait in line for longer periods of time or leave certain ride lines to go elsewhere depending on their age, the outside temperatures, and the time of day. This allows Disneyland to add or subtract cars and personnel to better handle the crowds. Because of continual knowledge of the whole truth, managers know how many people on average attend the park each day of the week during each season, holiday, and special event. This allows customers to drive the business and determine the standards for daily service based on supply and demand.

Significant companies not only have technology in place to capture external customer feedback, but also cultures of trust and open communications that enable them to receive feedback from employees. The need for whole truth ultimately requires that businesses do the hard work of creating environments that engender a sense of commitment and even ownership on the part of employees, so that employees strive to make operations run optimally. Thanks to Disney's uniquely fun culture built around Hollywood performance (Disneyland's personnel department is called "casting," employees are "cast members," job descriptions are "scripts," uniforms are "costumes," etc.), Disneyland employees *want to* work smarter, harder, faster, and longer, doing whatever it takes to deliver an extraordinary customer experience, and helping managers get closer and closer to the whole truth.

Is your place of employment one of the greatest places to work in your area and in your industry? What can you do right now to improve the morale of your employees, so that they feel invested enough to give you the frank, whole-truth feedback your business needs? And what steps can you take to make yourself more approachable as a leader, so employees feel comfortable giving feedback to you that helps you fix what's broken?

The Bottom Line

Some things are true whether or not you believe them. Everybody is entitled to his or her own opinion, but nobody is entitled to the wrong facts. We shouldn't believe everything we think. Successful people obey the preparatory principle called belief. Significant individuals live the advanced, highest Law of Always Seeking the Whole Truth. Whole truth gives us the answers and responses we need to inspire, direct, guide, and supervise the execution of our tasks and the responsibilities of others. In an even deeper sense, a complete knowledge of where we came from, why we are here, and where we're going allows us to connect, not just converse; feel, not just see; listen, not just hear; do, not just believe; live, not just exist—and, ultimately, to transform ourselves and our organizations from successful to significant.

Four Suggested Action Steps to Learning Whole Truth

1. List the seven major areas of life: physical, mental, spiritual, emotional, social, financial, and familial. Immediately identify the feedback systems you currently have in place to measure your present level of performance in each area. Whatever your system is, increase your frequency of feedback. If your business still prints quarterly reports, change it to a monthly report; a monthly to every two weeks; a weekly to a daily. If you check to see how your kids are doing in school on a monthly basis, try doing it every two weeks. Guaranteed: Your ability to make informed decisions will increase immediately.

2. To practice avoiding confirmation bias, pick a controversial topic—for example, abortion, gun control, the Palestinian–Israeli conflict, or some other—reflect on your current beliefs,

and extensively research the opposite side of the issue. As you gather information, clearly separate emotion from fact and circumstantial evidence from opinion. Now write a short, one-page essay defending the opposite view from what you believe.

3. Look up the most influential people in American media, including the highest-level producers and decision makers on the air, the most talented writers and directors in television, the top editors at newspapers, magazines, publishers. Research their personal lives to discover the whole truth about their politics, theology, education, sexual orientation, family background, and personal wealth. Through this exercise, you will see why and how each of these powerful individuals sways the hearts and minds of the American people based on the stories they choose to cover and the guests they choose to interview on their programs. Guaranteed: You will forever be aware of the frightening reality and necessity to avoid confirmation bias in your own life and realize why we should never believe everything that we hear or think.

4. It's important to know the whole truth about getting a promotion. As great as your current knowledge and skills may be for your current job, are they the skills needed at the next level? The top sales professional doesn't necessarily make a great manager; an all-pro athlete rarely makes a great coach. To make sure you are prepared for advancement, first name two skills you currently excel in and plan how you can leverage those skills for promotion. Next, name two skills or knowledge sets

you will need at the next level and sign up for classes or informational interviews that will equip you to get that promotion. The whole truth? Success comes from working for the organization, but significance comes from working on yourself so that you are always prepared for more responsibility.

Focus on Winning Instead of Team

Winning isn't something that happens suddenly on the field when the whistle blows and the crowds roar. Winning is something that builds physically and mentally every day that you train and every night that you dream.

—EMMITT SMITH

Most of us who work as part of a team or are on teams have been led to believe that it's *all* about the team, and that there's "no 'i' in team." Strong team spirit alone is enough to yield success in business, sports, and life, right? No! In every competition, one team loses! Companies are going bankrupt as you read this, and they have a team. Most important for our purposes, a purely team-centric focus doesn't allow us to reach the hallowed ground of significance. For that, we must reflect back on our own attitudes and mind-sets, ensuring that as individuals making up the team, we're each pursuing a higher purpose: *winning.*

As we've seen so far in these chapters, the difference between preparatory success principles and the advanced, highest Laws of Significance essentially comes down to some combination of meaning, awareness, and purpose. This holds true here, too. Average people come together as merely a *group* or an assemblage of people with many personal hidden agendas. Successful people form themselves into more cohesive *teams* that can work together to achieve specific tasks. But teams in and of themselves don't mean all that much unless individuals on the team commit themselves to an ultimate purpose, which is *winning*. Winning is thus the higher Law of Significance built upon the preparatory success principle of team.

If you think about it, this highest law makes perfect sense. Winning at whatever game we are playing, whether at home, work, school, or in the military, is and always will be the reason we do what we do. If you don't agree, take down the basketball hoops at a Saturday-morning pickup game and see how many guys stick around just to run up and down the court for exercise. Keeping score is important, and winning gives our effort meaning. Even in our youth-sports programs, where out-of-touch parents don't keep score and give every kid a trophy, the kids circumvent this craziness by keeping score on their own. Without a scoreboard or official scorekeeper, at the end of every youth soccer match or T-ball game, the young players can tell you exactly how many goals were scored, by whom, and which team won. Unless we want to win, there is no reason to stretch or surround ourselves with people who can take us to a higher, better place than where we can take ourselves.

Yet winning, as I'm defining it here in connection with significance, is not just about what's on the scoreboard. Winning includes specific achievements, such as besting an opponent in a particular match or having a championship season, but in the highest sense, it is also about becoming everything you were born to be so that you can contribute to the team, which is now stronger with you than without you. Winning in the external world comes from the *inside;* it's ultimately personal and even spiritual. It entails excelling as a human being, not just achieving top technical performance. Champions *always* yearn to best their opponents, but they also know that they can win on a scoreboard and still be a loser. To have the best chance of winning on the scoreboard, we must surround ourselves with exceptional individuals—winners both on and off the field who are dedicated to the common cause.

Another way of putting this is to observe that winning in any competitive endeavor involves more than muscle and bone going through motion. It's about personal growth—going from where we are to where we want to be—and that takes heart, desire, discipline, drive, mental toughness, stern concentration, sacrifice of social life, hundreds of lonely hours of painful practice, and laserlike focus. At the beginning of every fiscal year, new season, or latest company product or service launch, we should ask ourselves: Are the members of our team committed winners, in both the literal and spiritual senses of the word? Are these coaches and players each in their own unique way significant enough to lead and inspire us to win the championship? Team Building 101 says if we can't change the players, *we change the players.* Whom must we let go or bring in, and what specific things must we change in order to nurture individuals' total commitment to realizing their human and technical potential, increasing in the process our team's chances of victory on the field?

Two "I"s in Winning

"It's all about team" apparently started when some insecure guy in an influential position failed so miserably that he wanted to relieve himself of personal responsibility for his poor performance, divert attention away from his weaknesses, and share the blame, shame, and painful loss with others. Consequently, his final excuse became the way-overused cry for unity, "There's no 'i' in team." Are you kidding me? If he wants to have a spelling bee, winning has two "i"s in it: The first represents Independent individual preparation; the second represents Interdependent collaboration. The teams that win on and off the field possess the greatest number of "i" players.

Even competitions that we regard as epitomizing team sports are ultimately, in a critical sense, driven by individual dedication and performance. I've been in Super Bowl and in NCAA Conference Championship team locker rooms right before the game begins, and the silent prayer of every athlete is: *Please don't let me be the weak link! No matter what, don't let me let my teammates down. Don't let me be the wimp who lets them run over me and past me to score the winning touchdown that defeats our team. A chain is only as strong as its weakest link, and please don't let it be me!*

Is soccer a team sport? World Cup teams like Manchester United and Real Madrid keep millions of fans across the globe enthralled. But with all due respect, it was superstars like Cristiano Ronaldo and the American-born and -bred goalie Tim Howard who made Manchester United unbelievable! Real Madrid's Robinho was amazing! Striker Thierry Henry made the French team incredible! Liverpool striker Robbie Keane was dominating! Manchester United then traded Ronaldo to Real Madrid, and he turned that team around. Real traded Robinho to Manchester City and helped them win. Lionel Messi turned Barcelona around and was named the FIFA World Player of the Year in 2009 and again in 2010.

Obviously, in soccer, players play for teams, but a team functions as a team only when one player passes to another. *Individuals* score and prevent goals. The entire game is played only by the one individual player who happens to have the ball in his or her possession and the one defender assigned to stop him or her at that one moment in time—until of course, a different offensive or defensive player takes over possession of the ball in the next successive moment in time.

Is baseball a team sport? In a televised ESPN Game of the Week, the batter hit a long fly ball to the multimillion-dollar-a-year Atlanta Braves outfielder. He caught the ball underhand, did a little moonwalk dance, flipped the ball up into the stands to the fans, and started trotting to the dugout. Cool? No! There were only two outs! The two runners on base couldn't believe their eyes and rubbed it in by skipping all the rest of the way to home plate to each score. The Braves manager was furious, fans were amused and incredulous, the outfielder's teammates felt angry and let down, and the ballplayer was humiliated. Individuals, not teams, determine who wins and who loses.

In the 2006 season of professional Major League Baseball, Minnesota Twins General Manager Terry Ryan was voted MLB Executive of the Year, and the Twins had all three American League individual award winners on their roster: Pitcher Johan Santana won the Cy Young Award for the second time in three years, Catcher Joe Mauer won the AL Batting Title, and First Baseman Justin Morneau was named AL MVP. Yet Minnesota didn't even make it into the World Series. Why? The team did not win enough games to reign as champions that year because only three out of nine starting players were legitimate "i" players.

This raises the obvious question: What about those teams that purchase a full roster of outrageously paid superstar players from the free-agent market yet still don't win a championship? My answer: "I" players are not necessarily all high-paid, big-name superstars. Winning teams also frequently have a certain number of less visible "i" players who understand the team's approach to playing and play their hearts out.

In 1984 the New York Mets drafted two future superstars, Darryl Strawberry and Dwight Gooden, right out of high school. In anticipation of their arrival, and understanding how difficult it can be for young players to adapt to stardom, the Mets management brought in an aging superstar, George Foster. In his heyday, Foster had been a five-time All-Star, a league-leading home-run hitter, and a National League MVP. But by the early 1980s, he had lost power at the plate and strength in his throwing arm. The Mets knew this, yet they gave Foster the largest contract in the league at that time. Why? Because Foster was an African American superstar who had the career stats and respect required to encourage Darryl and Dwight in their work ethic. Foster also just happened to be a devout Christian who would serve as a conservative role model, voice of reason, and disciplined big brother off the field. Foster was the perfect, specialized "i" player the Mets needed to keep these guys focused and out of mischief, which paid off big in 1986, when the Mets won the World Series.

The Ten Commitments

"I" players young and old are easily spotted, if you know what to look for. All "i" players understand, embrace, obey, and live by what I call the Ten Commitments. The first six "C"s correspond to the first "i" in winning—Independent Indiviual preparation—while the last four correspond to the second "i"—Interdependent collaboration.

Clarity, the first and most fundamental "C," involves defining who you are—personal authenticity—and knowing that you must first like yourself before you can like others, love yourself before you can love someone else, and trust yourself before you can trust anyone. Clarity is taking ownership and responsibility for every success and failure, knowing that success comes not from how you look or how you dress or how you're educated, but from how you think. Clarity is laser-like focus that cuts through life's clutter like a beacon through a thick night fog. Be you, everything you were born to be, for you'll make a lousy somebody else!

Character, the second Commitment "C," involves aligning beliefs with behavior, because if the things you think about diverge from the things you do, you will never be happy, successful, or significant. Having good character means establishing and obeying convictions. Character is moral excellence, firmness, and integrity, and as such it spawns and perpetuates trust. A person with character is mentally strong, emotionally awake, ethically straight, and committed to doing what is right, not what is easy.

Competence, the third "C" in the Ten Commitments that make "i" players winners, comes from practice and preparation. It has been said that if you are prepared, you shall not fear. If you are a skydiver, cockiness is feeling invincible for no reason and recklessly stepping out of the plane to land wherever the wind takes you. Competence involves confidently possessing the knowledge, technical skills, and experience required for the task at hand. It is carefully and methodically packing your chute so you feel invincible for every reason, and jumping out of the plane to land where you plan to land. Competence is synonymous with confidence, which allows some people and organizations to always land on their feet, even when others, equally talented, stumble again and again.

Consistency, the fourth Commitment "C," is performance free from variation or contradiction. You can't just turn excellence on and off. Consider the physical, mental, spiritual, emotional, financial, social, and family realms of your life. In which area of your life do you want to lose? In which area are you not becoming more of who you are and reaching your full potential? Winning is a way of thinking and believing, a way of life, and as such it knows no boundaries. At the deepest level, consistency is about caring about everything we do. In sports, we must care about our individual preparation for each game as well as for the welfare of all our fellow team members and their families. In business, we must care about our company, its performance, productivity, and profitability, and about our coworkers and their families. In the military, we must care about our brothers and sisters in arms and their families. By no means can we be perfect, but in the process of caring and of relentlessly pursuing perfection, we attain significance.

Competitiveness, the fifth Commitment "C," remains critical and essential to strong performance. As previous chapters have illustrated, significance doesn't entail competing with others, but with one's self. Competitive people in this sense relentlessly seek out their "physical therapists" of the body, mind, and spirit who stretch us to do what we've never done so we can get what we've never had. Competition in the spiritual sense is about ceasing to complain about challenges and instead embracing the values of creative adaptability, transformation, and modification. It's about finding the opportunity in change and altering thinking, strategy, and behavior before circumstances force us to.

Cause, the sixth Commitment "C," means focusing on service before self and remaining constantly aware of the why behind change and competition. Individuals, businesses, organizations, and teams who execute for one game or one sales cycle do so because they have become good or great or even best in the peripherals of success: blocking, tackling, throwing, catching, batting, putting, driving, typing, filing, selling, marketing, promoting, and delivering on quality and service.

In order to create a long-lasting, world-class business and a championship dynasty in sports, we must know and do more than the obvious outward peripheral endeavors. We must uncover the seeds that bring forth the fruits of conviction—in other words, a deeper purpose; a sense of cause.

Chemistry is the seventh of the Ten "C"s and is the transitional commitment that turns our team-building focus from Me to We. Although clarifying the cause individually and collectively helps us start a winning streak, nothing of a long-term nature will ever exist or sustain itself unless we have chemistry. The New York Yankees, the Washington Redskins, and the Los Angeles Lakers have all had at one time the highest salary base in their leagues, and yet they still could not win a championship. What was missing? That strong mutual attraction, those vibes that make the relationship click so that everybody says, "I like me best when I'm with you. I want to see you again." Yet chemistry can't emerge unless *each individual* moves beyond ego, jealousy, and possessiveness, realizing that doing so is necessary if we ourselves are to flourish as human beings. Chemistry means opening our hearts and minds to our teammates, seeing ourselves in them and them in us, and growing in the process into our best selves.

Contribution, the eighth "C," entails giving everything we've got when less would be sufficient—not because others expect it, but because we as individuals demand it of ourselves, and because doing so helps us to realize our potential. Total contribution breeds and sustains trust—our own trust first, then our teammates' trust—because we are giving maximum effort. Teams lose when superstar individuals merely try to win the game for their team. They win when a team of extraordinary "i" players comes together to do whatever is necessary to help each other succeed. All of us can and should take our attitudes, expectations, commitments, performances, and productivity to a higher level. No excuses. Victory is always the goal and the reason we never stop hustling. It doesn't matter how tall or short we are, whether we are male or female, how much we weigh, or if we're fast or slow—every one of us can hustle. Everyone can give more, serve more, work harder and smarter, and become more of who we already are. Commitment to total contribution (especially during practice) allows us to always rise to the occasion, which in turn inspires our teammates. All of us together become the players we were born to be.

Cooperation, the ninth Commitment "C," is chemistry in action, especially during difficult times. Cooperation means listening without judgment, appreciating that a group can congeal only through conflict. When strong cooperation exists, team members pull through disagreements and emphasize through word and deed that we are one—we live together and we die together. At the same time, cooperation means individuals are unafraid to express their opinions, knowing that opposing viewpoints force the team to improve. Cooperating teammates don't all think the same thing, but they focus on what is right instead of on who is right, knowing that if two people agree on everything, one of them is not necessary. Each individual is the cohesive glue that binds together the team for the benefit of the team's higher purpose. And individuals cooperate because they also recognize that the team is a vehicle for their own personal growth and development. As the team wins, both the team and the individuals reach their greatest potential.

Conclusion, the tenth and final Commitment "C," means we will finish together, focusing on the acronym WIN (*What's Important Now*) until each of us gets our desired result, which is winning. Conclusion comes when we remember that it's not enough to say, "I will do my best." We must succeed as individuals at doing what is necessary, understanding that when the water in the lake goes up, all boats rise together. Conclusion entails loyalty first to oneself and our own convictions, then to a cause, and finally to our teammates. With a commitment to conclusion, team members become loyal to those who are not present, never gossiping or backbiting. Most people define loyalty as a noun: Something to which one is bound by a pledge or duty. I think of loyalty as a verb: That which sustains the team members so that they can conclude what they started.

No Compromise

Notice I have not mentioned compromise as one of the Ten Commitment "C"s. Compromise has no place in building a winning team.

In sports, we know that momentum lasts only as long as your next play, and that once you find a momentum shifter (like a blocked kick or a goal line stand), what you do on the very next play allows you to take advantage of this newly captured momentum. Why would anyone want to give up this competitive advantage just to make it fair and make sure no one feels bad so they keep playing the game?

We normally negotiate a compromise on a linear plane: You give up something and I give up something, and we meet in the middle, weaker than we were by ourselves, just so we can stay together. It's like the second law of thermodynamics, where you put a hot substance in the same vat with a cold substance and within minutes they morph into an average warm temperature. Even more problematic, compromise is about who is right and holding on to whatever you can. Are you kidding me? I thought change and winning was not about who is best, but about *what is right*. Significant people obey higher, universal laws whether it's in their selfish interest or not. Do we merely live by situational ethics, selective integrity, service for self, and excellence in only a few things we do? Absurd!

Zen Buddhists never compromise, and they are the most peace-loving people on our planet. They envision negotiating as an equilateral triangle where each party begins at one end of the base and moves upward toward the triangle's apex. Moving closer and closer to becoming one at the top, the parties have become stronger together than they were apart. By letting go of *I'm right* and focusing on *we're right*, we still meet in the middle, but it's a higher middle that Buddhists call the Way.

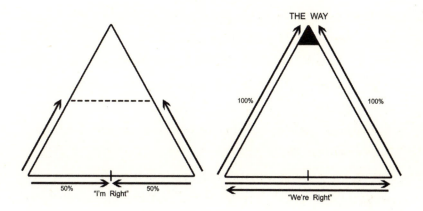

These triangle templates clearly show that in any relationship, if each of the two parties gives only 50 percent, it is literally impossible for them to connect at a higher level. However, when each party gives 100 percent to the relationship, they connect at the highest physical, mental, emotional, and spiritual points possible, where they become more of who they already are and can accomplish more together than apart.

Do you tend to compromise in your daily work or in your relationships at home? Have you watered down the principles to which you claim to subscribe? Looking hard at the way you resolve conflict with others, are you simply pursuing self-interest and protecting your turf, or do you go the extra mile to create an entirely new, elevated reality with your partner in conflict?

Lessons from the NFL

The Ten "C"s allow us to distinguish between good or great performance and truly significant, legacy performance. The best or the greatest coaches and players possess maybe four "C"s: clarity, competence, consistency, and competitiveness. But the best leaders, managers, coaches, and players don't win championships—significant ones do! The best and greatest coaches and players can win on any given day and become successful in the short term, but winning "i" players achieve the highest level of significance, which in turn creates and sustains a long-term dynasty.

On some teams, players live by only one or two of the "C"s. These teams are always in last place and struggling for team unity and organizational identity. During the early 1990s, the National Football League's Tampa Bay Buccaneers wallowed in last place as the worst team in professional sports—not just football, but basketball, badminton, even bowling! At the end of the team's 1994–95 season, which began with the death of owner Hugh Culverhouse and ended with the team's winning only two games, I visited the Buc's headquarters and got firsthand insight into why the team was losing.

As I entered the office, the receptionist seemed bothered that I was there. Refusing to get up and assist me, she buzzed me through the door. Behind her counter, I saw trash all over the floor and a table with four unmatched chairs around it. In the corner of the meeting room stood a stack of four old Pizza Hut boxes. And when I interviewed the players, asking each one the same question—"Why are you here?"—not one player looked me in the eye. They all answered the same way: "I'm here to play football." The operative word being "I'm." It was obviously only a job to them, an egotistical, success-minded pursuit devoid of the meaning, purpose, and real spirit that accompany a winning effort. As I left the Buccaneers headquarters, clear to me was the fact that not a single person I'd met was living by the Ten "C" Commitments, and I also found little evidence of the stretching required to raise players' personal and organizational broomsticks. I couldn't help but reflect on the silent prayer of every "i" player—*Please don't let me be the weak link.* Unfortunately, most of their players and employees at every level were.

Compare my visit to the Buccaneers with my visit to the Super Bowl Champion Dallas Cowboys in the same season and in the same week. When I entered the Cowboys headquarters to work with their team, everything was glass, brass, crystal, and leather, and everything was perfectly in its place. The sophisticated receptionist personally escorted me into the meeting room. When I interviewed the Cowboys players and asked them the same question—"Why are you here?"—each of them stood up tall and straight, looked me square in the eyes, and with emotion proudly stated, "We're here to win the Super Bowl!" Notice their operative word: "We're." They had won back-to-back championships, Super Bowl XXVII in 1992 and XXVIII in 1993, but failed in 1994. They felt they simply needed someone to help them regain focus on the Ten "C"s and hold them accountable. Because they were all living by and obeying at least seven of the Ten "C"s, the Cowboys won Super Bowl XXX as a unified team of "i" players and coaches.

An interesting coda: A few seasons later, the NFL hired a nonpartisan, independent survey company to measure the level of commitment of players on the previous year's top two teams and bottom two teams. The plan was simply to phone the players on their day off to see what they were doing. When players on the AFC and NFC Champion Super Bowl teams were called, they were found exercising or working at the headquarters office, doing something to better themselves and their team. When players on the two last-place teams were called, they were still home in bed. Think of your team at work. How many true "i" players do you have? And how many members of your team are merely "best" players, individuals who may perform well technically but who lack heart, tenacity, and commitment? What kind of player are you? Are you *in the way* or *on the way* to helping your team win? Are you part of the problem or part of the solution? Does your attitude divide the team or unify it?

The Bottom Line

Successful people build teams and think strictly in terms of team spirit. When significant people compete, they keep in mind the greater purpose of competition, which is to win. Winning is a mentality pursued and possessed by *individuals* that gives rise in turn to superior team performance. On a winning team, each member takes ownership and makes winning personal, speaking of "my" team, not of "our" team. Winning takes place on the field, but all on-the-field wins originate in the individual's off-the-field commitment—in the grit, determination, honor, integrity, focus, and sacrifice each of us shows when we try our hardest to jump higher and move beyond where we already are, technically, emotionally, and spiritually. Winning on both the individual and collective levels is really the only reason for assembling a team, and winning begins and ends with significant individuals who are deeply committed to developing their own selves.

Four Suggested Action Steps to Building a Winning Team

1. Anyone can become an inspirational leader of a team, no matter where he or she is on the organizational chart. The key is

to inspire others through example by demonstrating your commitment to becoming a winning player. Set aside a little bit of time every day to personally work on one of the Ten Commitments. Get somebody on the team to help support you as you stretch. This person will likely share his or her experience with your peers, who in turn will be inspired by your high level of dedication.

2. Interview every single candidate who could serve as a possible player on your team. Your screening process will rate candidates not merely on the basis of their education or the specific skill set required for the position, but also on the basis of the person's apparent understanding of the importance of the Ten Commitments. Create a list of leading questions that require more than just a yes or no response and that will allow you, as the interviewer, to evaluate which of the Ten "C"s the candidate possesses and is currently living.

3. Identify the exact number of players required to build your winning team, triple that number, and invite these individuals to a multiday tryout situation or to a one- or two-week internship. With this you can actually see which of the Ten "C"s are automatic in their performances. Discover which of the candidates knows who they are, makes everybody else around them better, and are predictable enough to trust.

4. Evaluate the families, friends, and affiliations of prospective team members. Interview past educators and coaches or employers to find out the truth about your prospects' attitudes and ability to perform under pressure.

Law 7

Do Right Instead of Seeking to Be Best

Place me behind prison walls—walls of stone ever so high, ever so thick, reaching ever so far in the ground—there is a possibility that in some way or another I may be able to escape. But stand me on that floor and draw a chalk line around me and have me give my word of honor never to cross it. Can I get out of that circle? No, never! I'd die first!

—KARL G. MAESER

Successful individuals may strive to be "great" or "best," but significant people go further and aim to *do right*, even, and especially, when that is the harder path. We need to discipline ourselves to always do the right thing, simply because it is the right thing to do. Knowing what is right and doing it involves subscribing to universal laws and core values not influenced by economics, passion, politics, or anger. It also entails remaining mindful at all times of our larger, spiritual purpose as human beings.

It is precisely right, ethical conduct—rather than mere technically proficient, "best" conduct—that allows significant people to lead and inspire others. President Dwight D. Eisenhower remarked that "leadership is the art of getting someone else to do something you want done because he wants to do it." Such a feat occurs only when subordinates actually believe we are the right person, in the right place, at the right time, for the right reasons, so we can and will do what's right.

Should we really give up trying to be "great" or "best" in order to do right? Doing best is short term and can win a game on any given day, but it can't win championships. Best can make a sale, but it can't gain loyal customers and increase long-term market share. When we make being the best our goal, we often don't wind up doing the right thing. But when doing right becomes our goal, we usually wind up being the best at what we do.

Once we become best, something surprising happens: We find that life's ultimate accomplishments derive not from competing against others (as the concept of "best" implies), but from measuring up to the highest possible standards of performance—those defined by our own consciences and the universal laws naturally inscribed in them. True satisfaction, meaning, and joy come from doing the noble and honorable thing—and not just when it's convenient, but all the time. When we finally resolve those nagging conflicts between our beliefs and our actions, we can find the peace within ourselves that we've worked for and the reconciliation with others that we have always sought. It is from this higher ground that we transform ourselves and our organizations from successful to significant and become *right*.

Doing Right in Spite of Our Feelings

Some might wonder whether universal standards of right conduct really exist, and if they do, whether we have access to them. I have studied and interviewed many of the most significant individuals in business, education, sports, and the military, and the one thing they hold in common is the conviction that no matter what, we must always do the right thing, simply because it's the right thing to do. Such people seem happy, confident, and peaceful, and I think it's because they are keyed in to the universal notions of right behavior contained in their consciences, and because what they believe in their heart of hearts conforms to what they do.

Once while I was an invited guest on a live television talk show in Stamford, Connecticut, the hostess commented, "So, you are an author and speaker, which makes you a perceived expert. Who said your values are the right ones? Who gave you the right to impose your core beliefs on any of us? Who put you in charge of telling us what is right?"

She blindsided me, but I found her questions provocative and welcome. "You are absolutely correct," I answered. "I do not, nor does anyone, have the right to impose my values on anybody. For some reason, many equate values with religion and immediately get their knickers in a twist. I fully understand the separation of church and state and will always obey, honor, and sustain the laws of every land. It's never about *who* is right, but *what* is right. Let's not talk about *my* values; I never do anyway. What values do you *not* want me to teach? Charity, forgiveness, honesty, love, acceptance, human rights with equal responsibility, hard work, integrity, service, excellence?"

Although this interview lasted a mere ten minutes, my off-the-cuff comments calmed her indignation and stirred within me a realization that some things are true and right—*period*. When people make decisions based on the feelings of a crowd, they end up with the flip side of the "confirmation bias" mentioned in the chapter on seeking whole truth. Whereas confirmation bias happens when people in power use their positions of authority to influence and sway private and public opinion to suit their personal agendas, *argumentum ad populum* (Latin for "appeal to the people") is the fallacious argument that a proposition is true because most of the people believe it. In other words, if many believe so and say so, it is so. Even though an argument may feel right if many people think it, the number of people who subscribe to it is not an indication of the validity of the argument.

Morally correct, right answers represent timeless, pure truths that transcend political, geographic, and socioeconomic conditions. They have always been and will always continue to be absolutely right. We cannot vote right into existence, agree to it by consensus, or rationalize and intellectually explain it away. Right is the strong, stable, secure lead car on the roller-coaster ride that stays on track regardless of ups, downs, twists, and turns—reminding us that the only one who gets hurt on a roller coaster is the one who jumps off. Each generation tries to disregard right answers, calling them old fashioned and out of sync with popular fads and new theories, but no matter how hard anyone tries, these answers remain simple, pure, valid solutions to twenty-first-century challenges.

It's unfortunate that with global competitive pressures mounting, the once traditional do-what's-right approach to personnel management has become obsolete, with corporations seeming to emphasize only what's best. I invite you to ask yourself: Are you usually right in your professional conduct? You can make a profit, win an athletic competition, or win a battle by being great and best, but you cannot make a difference, win a championship, or win the war unless you are right. If right is possible, then great really is not good enough.

A Cautionary Tale

I'd like to help you discern the difference between right and best by offering different perspectives or angles on making right decisions and living in an upstanding, "right" way. I'll begin by observing that when we forget about right and grasp onto an image of "best," we pay the price, as the saga of America's Olympic basketball team suggests. After America won a bronze medal in the 1988 Olympics with nonprofessionals, the Olympic Committee changed the eligibility rule, allowing professionals to compete. Starting with the 1992 Barcelona Olympics, the USA has consistently fielded a "Dream Team" made up almost exclusively of NBA all-stars—classy human beings like Michael Jordan, David Robinson, Karl Malone, and John Stockton. However, in the 2004 Summer Olympic Games in Athens, Greece, things went horribly wrong. Again made up of a league of NBA all-stars, this so-called Dream Team managed to lose three games—more losses in a single year than the country's Olympic basketball teams had suffered in all previous Olympic games combined. The world will never forget the media coverage of how these indignant, arrogant players behaved disrespectfully to the locals and other athletes and tarnished the integrity of the game that had granted them their fortune and fame. One bold *USA Today* headline pulled no punches when it printed "Not Even 680 Million Dollars Could Buy the USA a Gold Medal!"

Because of this disastrous outcome, the American men's basketball team changed its philosophy and is now focused on fielding a team of significant, right-living players as opposed to simply sending a bunch of the best prima donnas. As a result, Team USA won a gold medal at the 2008 Olympics and then again in 2012, once again restoring America's pride and dignity. This episode recalls another one involving the legendary 1980 U.S. hockey team. When asked how he could possibly know he had selected the best players in only one tryout practice, Coach Brooks replied, "I don't want the 'best' players; I need the twenty-two 'right' players if we are to beat the Russians and win Olympic gold!" He did get the right players, and the rest is history.

How do you get the right players? The following chart diagrams the steps required to identify, attract, and retain the right people in sports, education, business, and the military. When one is the right person (living by all Ten Commitment "C"s described in the previous law), it is natural to attract other right people committed to creating and sustaining right relationships. Together, these people inspire one another to seek the right training, which teaches them to act on right reasons. This creates situations where the right leaders, who know the necessity of giving their people the right tools and who empower each person with the right authority to take personal responsibility for his or her actions, emerge. People with the right authority engage in the right practices, which almost guarantee that everyone will reap personal and organizational right rewards.

The Nine Rules of Right

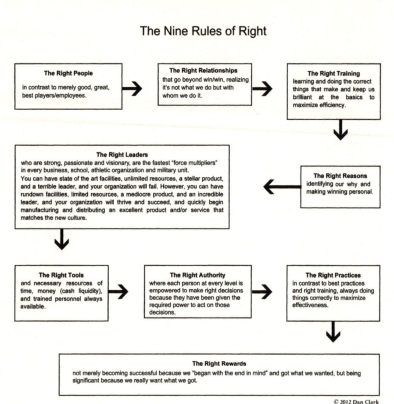

The Right People
in contrast to merely good, great, best players/employees.

The Right Relationships
that go beyond win/win, realizing it's not what we do but with whom we do it.

The Right Training
learning and doing the correct things that make and keep us brilliant at the basics to maximize efficiency.

The Right Leaders
who are strong, passionate and visionary, are the fastest "force multipliers" in every business, school, athletic organization and military unit.
You can have state of the art facilities, unlimited resources, a stellar product, and a terrible leader, and your organization will fail. However, you can have rundown facilities, limited resources, a mediocre product, and an incredible leader, and your organization will thrive and succeed, and quickly begin manufacturing and distributing an excellent product and/or service that matches the new culture.

The Right Reasons
identifying our why and making winning personal.

The Right Tools
and necessary resources of time, money (cash liquidity), and trained personnel always available.

The Right Authority
where each person at every level is empowered to make right decisions because they have been given the required power to act on those decisions.

The Right Practices
in contrast to best practices and right training, always doing things correctly to maximize effectiveness.

The Right Rewards
not merely becoming successful because we "began with the end in mind" and got what we wanted, but being significant because we really want what we got.

Overcoming Obstacles

Bill Greehey grew up in a home with a roof over it but not much more. Bill's father worked for minimum wage in the gypsum mill, and his mother ran a tiny, unsuccessful bakery. Bill worked at his mother's business from the time he was twelve years old and earned extra money for the family by shucking corn at local farms. When he was fifteen, like every other young man his age in Fort Dodge, Iowa, Bill went to work part time at the gypsum mill to provide further support for his family. For a young man of sixteen the expectation was that he would quit school to work full time at the mill, and that's where he would one day retire. Going against his father's wishes, Bill graduated from high school and was the only member of his graduating class—and the only person ever from his small town—to attend college.

Bill subsequently became the longtime CEO of Valero Energy and is the current chairman of NuStar Energy, which has its headquarters in San Antonio, Texas. Because of his childhood experience, Bill developed a corporate culture at Valero and NuStar of encouraging the less fortunate and giving back to the community. Under his leadership, Valero was ranked fifteenth on the Fortune 500 for corporate philanthropy. Bill transferred that culture to the Valero spinoff, NuStar, where in 2009 alone the company's 1,750 employees contributed over 60,000 hours volunteering for nonprofits in communities where the company operates.

Bill believes leaders can't just talk about a culture of giving. We must lead by example and provide opportunities to others to see and feel the difference between working hard to successfully make a living and working hard to significantly make a difference. At Valero and NuStar, top executives get involved in every volunteer project the companies undertake.

Valero and NuStar themselves benefit from their culture of giving. NuStar is ranked twenty-one on the Fortune 500 list of "The 100 Best Companies to Work For"; in 2006, when Bill retired from the company, Valero was number three. As he puts it, "When employees are involved in the community financially and giving of their time, they feel good about working at a company that encourages and supports that activity. Most companies think shareholders come first.

I believe if you put your people first, they will take care of the share-holders, and they'll care more about the company." The numbers bear him out. When Greehey took over as CEO of Valero, it was a debt-ridden organization. When he retired, it was the largest inde-pendent petroleum refiner and marketer in North America.

NuStar separated from Valero in 2007, and Greehey stayed on as chairman of NuStar. Since 2001 NuStar has grown from 160 employ-ees to 1,750 today; from less than $400 million in assets to $5.1 bil-lion; and from $46 million in net income to over $224 million in 2008. Greehey attributes all of this growth and prosperity to a cor-porate understanding of the difference between becoming successful and being significant.

The crown jewel of Greehey's extraordinary personal philan-thropy is Haven for Hope, a most unusual center benefiting the homeless. Haven for Hope is a nonprofit dedicated to transforming and saving the lives of homeless men, women, and children by ad-dressing the root causes of homelessness through education, job training, and fully funding a detoxification facility center and coun-seling center to help the mentally ill. For those who are not ready to get back into society, Haven provides the Prospects Courtyard, just outside the main campus, where individuals can get clothing and showers, along with medical and dental attention.

A model for how to deal with homelessness, Haven for Hope has already been visited by representatives from two hundred cities around the United States who want to do something significant with their lives and resources.

Overcoming Ego

When we fall prey to a glitzy image of "best," often our egos are doing the talking. Behaving rightly requires that we overcome ego and
the small-minded parts of us for the sake not merely of long-term
results, but of larger principles. When leaders manage to do so—
when they behave charitably and compassionately—they inspire
others and leave real legacies to their descendants.

In April 1865, Generals Ulysses S. Grant and Robert E. Lee met at
Appomattox Court House to negotiate the peace treaty ending the Civil
War. Grant had just seized Richmond and the war was virtually over.
Grant could have behaved egocentrically, thinking only short term as
the conqueror, humiliating the Confederacy by knocking them to their
knees and stomping on them while they were down. Instead, Grant
treated the Confederate Army right—with dignity and respect. Thinking long term, he allowed the Confederate officers to keep their guns
and the soldiers to keep their horses, and he released all of them with a
full day's supply of food and rations to help them return home to their
loved ones. When word of these surrender terms spread throughout the
North and the South, the healing and reuniting of sick and broken
America began. All Americans benefited, not only because Grant did
the best thing for America, but because he did the right thing.

In 1981, under very different circumstances, America's leaders
again checked their egos and did the right thing as American automobile manufacturer Chrysler Corporation teetered on the brink of
bankruptcy. Chrysler's CEO, Lee Iacocca, went before the U.S. Senate
and requested $1.2 billion in guaranteed government loans. A lot of
Americans didn't think this was best or right. Philosophical concerns

about free markets aside, it might have felt tempting to punish Chrysler for poor decision making, standing by as the company got its just punishment. Iacocca explained that if the government did not bail out Chrysler, the company would end up paying $2.7 billion in welfare and unemployment to more than 500,000 Chrysler workers when the company folded. As we know, the government made a loan in 1984, and Chrysler made the final $800 million payment on the loan seven years early.

Do you ever fall prey to the impulse to "stick it" to your antagonists at work, just because you can? Does your company collaborate with competitors at important moments, or does it rub its competitors' noses into the mud when they're down? In the long run, overcoming the urge to say "I told you so" or "I'm better than you" yields the best result for everyone, and we walk away knowing that we behaved nobly in the most dire, decisive, and defining of moments.

Risking Everything for What's Right

Doing right not only wins Olympic gold, heals divided countries, and leads to superior financial results; it produces remarkable personal acts of heroism and valor. U.S. Air Force General David Goldfein was a young colonel in 1997 when he left his beautiful wife and two young daughters at an Air Force base in Europe to fly a bombing mission over Serbia. The war had been blazing for days, and Goldfein had already flown many sorties over Kosovo. He and his squadron of F-16C fighter jets had brought Kosovo under control and now turned their attention to Serbian leader Slobodan Milošević. Serbia possessed hundreds of surface-to-air-missile (SAM) sites dotting the countryside. Even flying at the usual 20,000 feet, the U.S.-led UN coalition forces were vulnerable because SAMs can reach 30,000 feet.

Strangely, the air base was so close to the war that families were deployed with the troops and lived as a community. Pilots would have dinner at home, go fight the bad guys, and return to base to sleep in their own beds. They would wake the next morning with their families and do it all again the next night, night after night until the mission was completed and the war was over.

On one bombing mission at 2 a.m., Goldfein had just unloaded his ordnances and was returning to base when a SAM hit his plane. Goldfein, whose call sign was "Fingers" (as in James Bond's Goldfinger), was at 20,000 feet going 450 knots and losing altitude and airspeed fast. The amazing F-16 remained flyable, but Goldfein still faced fire as he was coming down, smoke and flames shooting from his tail. At 10,000 feet, he pulled the nose up to give the aircraft a better trajectory as he bailed out, hoping the plane would continue much farther and put more distance between where he landed and where the plane crashed. The enemy always checked the wreckage first for the pilot. If he was captured, he knew he would most likely be tortured and dragged through the streets of Belgrade.

Goldfein's F-16 soared for another four and a half miles, and when he ejected he went pretty much straight down. Landing with only a few minor shrapnel cuts and bruises, he eluded the enemy for two hours until his rescue by a Blackhawk helicopter crew. At a safe airstrip, he boarded a C-130 and flew back to his fighter squadron base. The base commander and fellow squadron members knew he had been shot down and were worried. A quiet, tense numbness permeated the base. Can you image what his wife and children were going through? It wasn't until 4 a.m. that word came in that Goldfein was alive, and it would be at least 7 a.m. before he arrived back at the base and his health condition became known.

When Goldfein landed and walked off the big airlift plane, he received cheers, hugs, and high-fives from fellow squadron members assembled on the flight line. His wife and daughters ran and greeted him with hugs, kisses, and tears of joy. What a reunion! Given the late hour, David could only spend a few precious moments with his reunited family before he tucked his little girls in bed and said good night to his amazing and supportive wife. When morning came, they all shared breakfast, he took his girls to school, spent the entire day with his wife, and, as usual, read his daughters some bedtime stories that night before he tucked them in again. Suddenly it was his moment of truth. He was the squadron commander, all eyes were on him, and the mission brief was about to begin.

In the military, if you're shot down and don't feel like flying anymore, you're off the hook with a desk job. At a minimum, because almost losing your life is such a traumatic experience, downed pilots are grounded at least until doctors can check them out physically and emotionally. So what did Colonel Goldfein do? When most would have thought only about themselves, Goldfein thought only of others, the importance of the mission, and his part in fighting and winning the war. His father had been a fighter pilot, and his older brother, a two-star general, was also an F-16 fighter pilot. His nephew had recently graduated from the U.S. Air Force Academy and was training to fly F-16s. His entire family understood the fighter pilots' mantras: "*Libertas Vel Mors*—Freedom or Death." "Mission First, People Always." "Let's Roll!"

That night, Goldfein's loyalty to the U.S. Air Force's three core values—Integrity First, Service Before Self, and Excellence in All You Do—were put to the ultimate test. Were they mere words or a way of living life to the fullest? At midnight, with all of the pilots' wives gathered at the Goldfein home, David climbed into his newly assigned jet, saluted his crew chief and maintainers, and taxied down the runway to take off. In a sign of deep respect, admiration, and support, more than three hundred people from all over the base—cooks, engineers, security guards, doctors, nurses, transportation specialists, teachers, mechanics, secretaries, NCOs, and fellow officers—assembled and stood at attention on the side of the runway. Twenty-four F-16Cs took off—one every twenty seconds—and Colonel Goldfein again led them on their bombing mission. He radioed to each pilot that his home was twenty degrees to the left of the runway and reminded them that all the wives were gathered there. He said at wheels up to follow him on a flyby right over the ladies, who would all be outside waving and sending their hopes, love, and prayers for their safe return.

They flew that night, again into harm's way, to execute several dangerous missions, including destroying the very SAM sites that shot him down, and returned. Every night from then until the end of the war in Kosovo and Serbia they flew and did their duty. Colonel David Goldfein, who at this writing is a three-star lieutenant general and numbered Air Force commander, is a true hero to me, his coworkers, his family, and other freedom-loving people who know of his bravery and dedication to do what is right—when and where it is right.

A Circus Lesson

Living each moment to the fullest brings us closer to significance by enabling our natural goodness to come out, so that we make right choices that help and inspire others. In this respect, our relationships with our kids aren't just home life—they're a prime opportunity to express our highest selves.

When I was a young boy, Dad and I were standing in line to buy tickets for the circus. Finally, there was only one family between the ticket counter and us. This family made a big impression on me. Eight children, all probably under the age of twelve. You could tell they didn't have a lot of money. Their clothes were not expensive, but they were clean. The children were well behaved, all of them standing in line, two-by-two behind their parents, holding hands. They were excitedly jabbering about the clowns, elephants, and other acts they would see that night. One could sense that they had never been to the circus before. It promised to be a highlight of their young lives.

The father and mother led the pack, proud as could be. The mother held her husband's hand, looking up at him as if to say, *You're my knight in shining armor.* Basking in the humble realization that he was finally able to do something special for his kids, the man looked back at his wife with that swaggered look of, *Yes, I am the stud you married.* The ticket lady asked the father how many tickets he wanted. He responded, "Please let me buy eight children's tickets and two adult tickets so I can take my family to the circus."

The ticket lady quoted the price.

The wife let go of her husband's hand and dropped her head. The man's lip began to quiver. He leaned a little closer and asked, "How much did you say?"

The ticket lady again quoted the price. The man didn't have enough money. How was he supposed to turn and tell his eight kids that he couldn't take them to the circus? Seeing what was going on, and to ensure this father's pride remained intact in front of his family, my dad put his hand into his pocket, pulled out a $20 bill, and dropped it on the ground. (We were not wealthy in any sense of the word!) My father reached down, picked up the bill, tapped the man on the shoulder, and said, "Excuse me, sir, this fell out of your pocket."

The man knew what was going on, and it was obvious that he appreciated the help in a desperate, heartbreaking, embarrassing situation. He looked straight into my dad's eyes, took my dad's hand in both of his, squeezed tightly onto the bill, and with his lip quivering and a tear streaming down his cheek, replied, "Thank you, thank you, sir. This really means a lot to me and my family."

My father and I went back to our car and drove home. We didn't go to the circus that night, but we didn't go without. I am so thankful that I was raised by parents who taught me that we find meaning in life when we pour all of ourselves into every encounter, doing the right thing even when we are off the job and believe that nobody is watching.

No Regrets

It is not enough to intend to do right; we must actually do so *right now!* And if we do, we can die—as we all eventually will—feeling no regrets for how we lived. I learned this myself during a near-death experience I had that changed my life forever. I was flying from Dallas, Texas, to Salt Lake City on an old Boeing 727, a two-hour-and-fifteen-minute flight. As I boarded and settled into my seat, I noticed a gentleman sitting next to me reading a newspaper account of the United 727 jetliner that crashed in Iowa in 1989, killing hundreds of passengers. Looking over his shoulder, I read that failure in the hydraulic system had caused the crash. The pilots had lost their ability to steer the aircraft.

I fell asleep at takeoff and awoke thirty minutes later when the pilot came over the PA system. "I'm sure you've noticed that we are lumbering in the sky about seven thousand feet above the ground still on the outskirts of Dallas," he said. "We have lost the hydraulic steering system on the aircraft. We will remain airborne for another hour and a half to burn off excess fuel. Then we will attempt an emergency landing."

From my window seat, I looked down at the ground, thinking, *This could be it! I always thought that I would die of old age on a golf course. But no. I'm going down in a plane crash and only have a couple of hours to live.*

If you knew you were going to be involved in a fatal automobile accident in the next two hours, whom would you call? What would you say? I reached for the air-phone on the back of the seat in front of me, entered my credit card, and dialed the first telephone number I thought of—my mother. When she answered, she asked if phoning her from a plane was expensive. When I answered yes, she scolded me and wanted to hang up immediately to save money. I called out, "Wait, wait, I need to talk now."

I couldn't tell her I was going to crash because she would have probably interrupted with a mom-ism like, *Do you have on clean underwear?* I didn't tell her of the plane's predicament, but I did say I had been thinking and feeling many things for quite some time and decided not to forgo saying them any longer or ever again. I thanked her for going without a new dress so I could have the best football cleats and for postponing family vacations so I could stay home to play on an all-star baseball team—simple things that she thought went unnoticed all those years. I told my mom I loved her and needed her. She cried, saying, "I love you too," and we hung up.

I then phoned my wife to tell her that I loved her. I thanked her for all the walks we took barefoot in the sand; and for all the intimate conversations we had just by holding hands; for the slow, tender kisses and for all of the hugs where she was the last one to let go. Fighting back my tears I again whispered "I love you" and hung up the phone.

I then phoned my older brother, sister, younger brother, and a couple of my dearest friends, engaging all of them in intimate, emotional, and appreciative conversations. Well, obviously we didn't crash, and that was refreshing (until I got the enormous phone bill; I just wanted to talk, not buy stock in the corporation!). I learned a vital life lesson: Not only should we do what's right in a moment of crisis by expressing love and appreciation to family and friends; we must do the right things throughout our lives, because you never know when your number is up. I now live a lifetime every day with the firm conviction that if we behave rightly, we will not have regrets for things we did; we will have regrets only for things we did not do.

The Bottom Line

Successful people obey the preparatory principle of being best. Significant individuals live the advanced, highest Law of Doing Right. Doing right is often difficult but always simple. We naturally know what's right by looking inward and honestly consulting our consciences; indeed, the standards of right conduct are universal, available to everybody in every socioeconomic, political, religious, or ideological circumstance. They are worth defending, even if it leads to war. President Ronald Reagan reminded us to do right when he stated, "America was founded on a dream, and now it's your turn to keep that dream moving. We've always reached for a new spirit and aimed at a higher goal. We've always been courageous and determined, unafraid and bold. Who among us wants to say we no longer have those qualities? . . . All we need to do is act, and the time for action is now!"

Four Suggested Action Steps to Always Doing Right

1. Write the following quote by Lao Tzu on a card and put it on your refrigerator door: "Watch your thoughts; they become words. Watch your words; they become actions. Watch your actions; they become habits. Watch your habits; they become character. Watch your character; it becomes your destiny. Love all, trust a few, do wrong to none. Transcend political correctness and strive for human righteousness." By checking this card several times a day, you'll remind yourself to consult your intuition and to do exactly what it challenges you to do.

2. When you face a major life decision, remember this: If the decision is right, you will know it in your mind and feel it in your heart. To obtain clarity, you need to block out all the noise of everyday life. Get away to a private location; take a few deep, cleansing breaths, close your eyes, meditate for a moment, study the situation in your mind, and verbally ask out loud for help in making the right decision.

3. Take time out each day to review your conduct. Ask yourself, Did it hurt anyone—including me? Was it fair? Did it violate the Golden Rule? Was I told that it was wrong? Did I feel bad when I did it? If your conduct didn't measure up, acknowledge it and behave differently in the future when similar situations arise.

4. Similar to the challenge I issued in Law 1 to write your own personal credo, this new challenge asks you to write your own Honor Code of Conduct. At both the United States Air Force Academy and the U.S. Military Academy at West Point, the incoming cadets swear to live by an honor code stating a minimum standard of ethical conduct. This code simply but powerfully reads:

We will not lie, steal, or cheat, nor tolerate among us anyone who does.

Cadets are considered the code's "guardians and stewards" and at graduation commit to living it for the rest of their lives, stating:

Furthermore, I resolve to do my duty and to live honorably, so help me God.

Cadets who live under the honor code regard it as a vital pathway toward ethical maturity, helping them to do right all their lives.

Now write your personal Honor Code of Conduct. Then live it, because it lives in you!

Experience Harmony Instead of Forcing Balance

Harmony is the analogy of contrary and of similar elements of tone, of color and of line, conditioned by the dominate key, and under the influence of a particular light, in gay, calm, or sad combinations.

—GEORGES SEURAT

We've seen that success is a destination, whereas significance is a path, a journey. A success mind-set focuses on goals, but significant people know that goals are but an excuse for the game we play *in between the goals.* This chapter zooms in on this *in between,* on the quality of our journey. Finding meaning to such an extent that we experience a constant, calming confidence. To enjoy the benefits of significant living comes not from doing, but from being; not from multitasking, as so many of us do, but from organizing our time in a more holistic way, and finding our flow and harmonizing with the continual melodies playing in the lives around us.

How do you allot your time? Do you divide your life into satisfying, meaningful moments, and the unsatisfying, unmeaningful

hours you must devote to create those satisfying moments? I hope
not. If the only satisfaction we get from work is our paycheck every
two weeks, what about the eighty hours we must put in to get it? It's
not enough to just make a living—we must make a life. It's not
enough to just let life happen to us—we must take charge of our days
and of our destiny.

It's true that in multitasking and juggling, we're at least conceiving of some portion of our time as meaningful. Yet harmony is by far
the higher law—a recognition that *every* moment should bring out
all of who we are. Champions don't slice and dice their time; they
press forward every moment with full awareness of their one, unify-
ing purpose, knowing that if they are not constantly pushing themselves to their ultimate capacity as human beings, someone else,
somewhere else, is. And when they meet this person, he will win. To
become more significant, we need to harmonize the diverse elements
of our lives and see everything we do at all times as meaningful and
conducive to our own, personal "why."

Balancing and Juggling

Most of us do seek a balance between a work life and our family life.
But we rarely achieve it because balancing work schedules with family time and civic responsibilities suggests an either/or proposition
that is both unreasonable and unacceptable. When we take time off
from family to spend more time at work, our family suffers, feeding
guilt and creating a dysfunctional environment. Similarly, when we
spend all our time with family and neglect our work, our careers

falter. Life is life, and we have only one to live. Multitasking sounds impressive but, in reality, it supports the misguided notion that we can *balance* our lives. Those who boast that they excel at multitasking are actually bragging that they are average at a lot of things. Most of the time when we multitask we confuse activity with accomplishment. We appear busy yet produce no benefit.

Perhaps the biggest consequence we pay with the satisfaction we take in multitasking is that we become blinded as to how rich and complete our experience of time *could* be minute to minute. Eventually multitasking's inadequacy haunts most successful people, without their quite realizing why. So, what do they do? They decide that they're going to stop reacting to things as they come and to take control of their lives. Instead of trying to do several things at once, they resolve to do one thing at a time—to *juggle* their priorities. *A-ha!* they think—the solution to obtaining the work-family balance they have long been seeking.

Juggling is definitely an improvement over multitasking. No matter how many balls a juggler has in the air, he can only control the ball in his hand. Once he lets go of the ball, he has relinquished control over that one until he catches the next to control that one. Is this not the perfect metaphor for dealing with stress, pressure, and a life that seems to be veering out of control? A juggler knows his priority—to focus only on the ball in his hand. If we think like a juggler, we will see that life really isn't as crazy as everybody claims.

If we are completely honest, we really have only four major balls to juggle. The *self* ball is made of a crumpled $100 bill. Do you want it? What if it is dropped and someone steps on it and grinds it into the ground with his shoe? Do you still want it? No matter what happened or what anyone did to this rolled-up, ball-shaped $100 bill, it did not decrease in value. It was and still is worth $100.

Many times in our lives we are dropped, crumpled, and ground into the dirt by the decisions we make and the environment within which we live and work. Though at times we feel worthless, no matter what happens to us, we never lose our value. A $100 bill is still a $100 bill, regardless if it's dirty, crumpled, worn, torn, smashed, wet, dry, old, new, dropped, or juggled. You are priceless! Failure is an event, not a person. There is a difference between the person and the performance. Being up is better than being down, but in either place you are worth the same!

The second ball is the *family* ball, which is made of glass. We drop it, and it breaks and shatters into many pieces that can rarely be repaired. It is imperative that we keep it in the air at all times and at all costs.

The third ball is the *job* ball, which is rubber. If we drop it, it will always bounce back—sometimes higher, sometimes lower, but it will bounce back. Even if it is stepped on and flattened, it squishes out the sides, trying to break free. When it is finally released, it immediately returns to its original shape and form, ready to bounce again. The rubber job ball reminds us that there is always a way. We just need to find it.

Ball number four is the *belief* ball, made of gold. It is heavy and bright and sheds light on the others. When we drop it, it leaves a dent, but it stays right where we left it, allowing us to pick it up and juggle it again and again, whenever we decide to. The miracle of the gold belief ball is that if we dent it, as we pick it up and start using it again, somehow the movement ("faith with works") eventually smooths out the dent, and, as we juggle it, the blemish vanishes, leaving no sign we ever dropped it.

In multitasking and juggling, we're at least conceiving of some portion of our time as meaningful. Juggling in particular leads us to understand that time can hold meaning, since it forces us to focus and concentrate on only one thing each moment. Yet juggling becomes tiring and ultimately impractical. It becomes mere work. Think of your own life: Do you ever get sick and tired of keeping all your balls in the air, whether at work or in your life as a whole? Have you wondered if there may be a better way?

Harmony

Harmony is a better, higher way, and in order to explain it, I must take you into the world of music. When asked how many notes there are in music, most respond with the number seven: A, B, C, D, E, F, G. This is incorrect but typical. In actuality, a piano has seven white keys *plus* five black keys, which constitute an octave of twelve notes. Overlooking the black keys results in cacophony, just as overlooking the little things around us often ruins the harmony in our lives. The first step to achieving harmony is to recognize all the notes.

The second step is to arrange the notes. Every song ever written has used the same twelve notes. The only difference between one song and another is the order in which the twelve notes fall and the timing and spacing between the notes. Some songs highlight fewer than all twelve, such as the three quick G's and long E-flat in the opening of Beethoven's Fifth Symphony, which could possibly be the most memorable musical phrase of all time. From just twelve notes comes the incredible music of Rachmaninoff, Schubert, Bach, Paul McCartney, John Lennon, and David Foster. Beethoven's symphonies, Chopin's études, Vivaldi's violin concertos, Pachelbel's Canon, and Mouret's Rondeau all convey exhilarating emotion; using only twelve notes, these compositions mysteriously move our mood toward the triumphant, the melancholy, and the joyous, inviting us at all times to feel.

I believe music is life personified, and I ask my audiences: "How wonderful would your life be if each of you, regardless of your profession, saw yourself as a musical composer, and no matter how many hit songs you had written, you greeted every new day as an opportunity to take the same twelve basic notes and write another hit song?" Then I ask, "What is the difference between a hit songwriter and a lousy songwriter—one with a significant career and the other merely successful at writing songs?" They have access to the same twelve notes. (And if they write the songs in English, they have access to the same twenty-six letters in the alphabet.)

For that matter, what is the difference between a significant banker and a successful banker? They have access to the same interest rates and economy. What is the difference between a significant sales champion and a successful sales professional, between creating a significant customer experience and delivering successful minimum-requirement customer satisfaction?

The answer is exactly the same for every instance and aspect of life. The differences between a significant individual who knows how to create harmony in his or her everyday experiences and a successful person caught up in balancing his or her life are passion, imagination, and creativity. The significant person doesn't just go through the motions: Remaining ever mindful of her inner purpose, she projects energy into each moment, adding life and spirit to the twelve lifeless notes. In other words: She lives *harmoniously.* Songs start with a melody—the tune we sing—but harmony gives the melody texture, depth, and color. Harmony refers to the sounding of two or more different pitches in unison that either echo or complement the melody line or provide a grounded accompaniment beneath the melody, embracing it with emotion. Harmony conveys that life and spirit, that energy, and when we live harmoniously, we don't merely act—we *sing.*

The only difference between an extraordinary corporate manager and an ineffective manager, an outstanding military leader and an average military leader, a great parent and a poor parent, a winning coach and a losing coach, a loving family and a dysfunctional family, a true performing artist and a mere singer, is that for the former every moment is purposeful and in a sense *the same moment,* witnessing the same heartfelt projection of our full attention and energy— our dedication to life with our whole being. What matters most is not what we do, but with whom we do it; not how we do it, but why we do it; not what happens to us, but what we do with what happens to us. Because the concept of harmony is about living each moment in life to the fullest as if it were our last, harmony far transcends the common metaphors of work-life balance and juggling most of us use to describe how we spend our days.

Passion, Imagination, and Creativity

I've offered a literal definition of harmony, but in music and in life, harmony remains an ineffable, almost magical, experience, and that's because it brings together three things simultaneously: passion, imagination, and creativity. When we concentrate all of our being in the moment to achieve significance, these three things combined are what we project. Let me define them in turn.

If you have *passion*, you don't just hear, you listen; you don't just have sex, you make love; you don't just touch, you feel; you don't just play an instrument, you become the instrument. You laugh longer, cry harder, connect deeper. Passion is an internal drive to always do something more—to feel absolutely everything you can possibly feel—to be fully alive. In interviewing actor Peter Fonda (son of Henry), I asked him to name the most intriguing person he had ever met. Peter said that as a young boy, he and his sister Jane were living with their father in a coastal town in Spain. Because his father was so busy making movies, Peter was usually left alone and feeling lonely. Consequently, he befriended an older gentleman—Pablo Picasso. The famous artist lived and worked just around the corner from Peter's house.

Peter told me of the many times he was in Picasso's studio, watching him curse in Spanish at the paint while he dug it from containers and slapped it on his palette. He would scream and point at it, calling it "ugly, worthless, good for nothing, stupid, and a ridiculous glob of vulgar crap!" Then, taking his brush and reverently speaking in French, he would whisper, praising and complimenting the paint as he applied it to the canvas: "You are beautiful, elegant. You are spectacular, breathtaking. I love you, *je t'aime, je t'aime!*" Picasso yelled angrily in Spanish at what the paint was, but he deeply celebrated in French what it was becoming. In every sense of the word, Picasso epitomized passion. Passion amounts to heart—not what we do, but why and how we do it.

Imagination is visualizing, thinking, having curiosity and child-like wonderment, seeing more than others see, reading between the lines, having insight (not just eyesight), and going beyond the map, just as Christopher Columbus did in 1492. Imagination is mind over matter. It's not changing what is but improving it, making it *more* of what it already is. We encounter imagination everywhere, in big and small doses. When I consolidated my six offices scattered across North America into one headquarters, I hired the incredible Laura to run my operation. After only two months, realizing how amazing she was, I told her she needed her own business card. Laura agreed but asked what her title would be. I said it didn't matter; just make one up. Five days later, the cards arrived. They read: LAURA CALCHERA, "SUPREME COMMANDER." Now, that's imagination!

Clearly, seeing isn't believing: Believing is seeing. Imagination is our ability to see the complete and comprehensive potential in ourselves and in each opportunity by always looking at life from an eighty-thousand-foot perspective. And no it is not limited only to seeing pictures in the mind. One can imagine a sound, taste, smell, physical sensation, feeling, or emotion. Training ourselves to readily use our imagination gives us the ability to combine all the senses, preview life's coming attractions, and embrace the observation of Edgar Allan Poe: "Those who dream by day are cognizant of many things which escape those who dream only by night."

Creativity is our ability to use the tools of any endeavor in new and appropriate ways. When we apply creativity, we arrange the stuff of our imagination into something that makes sense and works; we connect passion to heart and mind and take them all together to a place they cannot go by themselves. Thomas Edison had passion and imagination and continually rearranged what they produced as he pursued his goal of creating the lightbulb. By experimenting with thousands of possibilities, as the old but relevant tale is told, Edison failed more than most even tried, and eventually failed his way to success. My friend Bill Doré said, "If you continue to live in the past, your life will be history. Create your future from your future. When Edison invented the lightbulb, he didn't start by trying to improve the candle."

Let me emphasize again that passion, imagination, and creativity are not mutually exclusive traits developed in a specific order, one at a time. They are simultaneous traits that feed off each other to help us accomplish our goal, our purpose. Significant individuals know it is their responsibility to always bring all three traits to work, to their homes, to their neighborhoods and schools, and to their leisure time.

According to the Nielsen Company, the average person watches six and a half hours of television per day. Through my interviews, I've discovered that successful individuals have reduced this obsession down to three hours per day, while those living lives of significance watch only two hours a day, filling that extra hour studying a foreign language, learning to paint or sculpt, practicing a musical instrument, reading inspirational books, taking classes at a local college, listening to motivational CDs, and serving others in a charity.

In other words, passion, imagination, and creativity drive us to use every moment so that each moment serves our purpose and helps us to grow, to develop, and to become more of who we already are. As we project these three elements, as we experience harmony at all moments of our day, we move closer toward significance.

Incentive Motivation

What about professional life? Does harmonious, minute-to-minute living lead to significance there as well? Here's a story about a man who not only imbued his career with spirit, but created conditions so that others could do so, too. Jack Johnson is a husband, father, grandfather, community philanthropist, and hero to all who know him. The third-youngest of seventeen children, he grew up in a tiny town called Holden, Utah. After high school, he moved to Southern California, where he met and married his extremely smart, beautiful, and supportive sweetheart, Ruth. Jack started A-Core, his own diamond-drilling/concrete-cutting specialist company in 1972 with only one employee—himself—and built it into a multimillion-dollar global business with over three hundred employees and at one time as many as ten offices. When I asked Jack for his one-word description of success, his most important leadership quality, he smiled and replied, "Belief. You've got to believe in yourself. All things are possible if only you'll believe."

Probing deeper, I discovered that Jack regarded *incentive motivation* as the only way he as a leader could inspire employees to believe in themselves enough to improve personal performance. Instead of telling employees what to do, incentive motivation fires a desire within each individual employee to do the right thing. Employees don't merely show up and push listlessly through their workdays; they become invested emotionally in their jobs, performing with passion, imagination, and creativity, and yielding great results for the company. Achieving a sense of ownership at work, they bring significant behavior out from within, rendering it more in line with their own personal purposes.

At year end, Jack paid out $323,000 in employee bonuses. Instead of paying money out to the insurance companies, Jack lavished it on his people as a reward for and benefit of abiding by his incredible safety program. Jack inspires his workers who drive company trucks to believe that they can, in fact, become better and safer drivers. If they go the entire year without an accident, each driver earns $1,000. This "inspired" self-belief has resulted in an almost perfect, accident-free transportation department for many years. These drivers aren't just driving: They're driving harmoniously, paying extra attention, thinking of new ways to do their jobs better, taking pride in what they've accomplished, and, in general, approaching their workday with more passion and interest.

Jack offers other companywide incentive programs, including a push for wellness. He knows that a physically fit workforce is more productive with less illness and sick days taken. He can't force his employees to exercise, lose weight, and stop smoking, so he inspires his workers to believe in themselves by paying big bonuses for each pound lost. Jack also pays $1,000 to anyone who quits smoking, renewing the gift each year the person remains a nonsmoker. Is it any wonder A-Core has no employee turnover? A-Core employees have license to bring their own behavior out from within. They exercise and stop smoking because they *want* to, and this same positive energy infects everything else that they do. They feel empowered to reach new heights, to inject more of themselves into their everyday tasks, to go the extra mile. Time at work seems more special, more meaningful, and this spirit bleeds into home life, too. Passion, imagination, and creativity aren't the exception for these employees—they're the rule!

I should add that Jack seeks to hire people with intensity and a sense of purpose, and he doesn't give up when they temporarily lose their way. A few years ago, one of his employees got caught up in drug use and crime and spent several years in prison. When he was released he came to Jack looking for a job and a chance to start his life over again. Jumping at the opportunity to help him and his family, Jack hired him back. After two years, this man is now the heart and soul of the shop, always positive, enthusiastic, and arguably one of the most charismatic, creative, and inspirational leaders in the company. So far Jack has hired ten individuals who have had run-ins with the law, and each one has turned out to be a stellar employee. They believe in themselves—and exert themselves with passion, imagination, and creativity minute to minute—because Jack believes in them.

In 2006 Jack's appendix burst and he almost died. I know of no one who has ever had more people praying for his complete recovery and so deeply concerned for his welfare. As of this writing, Jack has handed out millions in companywide bonuses and incentive programs to his beloved employees, whom he treats as family. I love this man and take great pride in calling him my friend.

The Bottom Line

Successful people obey the popular preparatory principle called balance. Significant individuals live the advanced, highest Law of Harmony. Significant people don't chop up their time, whether by multitasking or juggling; instead, they live every moment in the same way, meaningfully, with their whole being and in alignment with their inner purpose. They pay attention and behave deliberately, knowing that quality and quantity of time is the price we pay for relationships, which, after all, are built one person, one moment, at a time. More specifically, significant people achieve harmony through a perfect blend of passionate love, imaginative work, and creative service. Aligning their inner purposes with their actions at all times, they discover a spirited, emotional existence, singing in everything they do, turning their lives into orchestral masterpieces that please themselves and delight all who hear them. Unless we consistently create opportunities to accomplish things we find important and meaningful, working to become better organized and balanced will only serve to fill up our time—and make us more frustrated.

Four Suggested Action Steps to Experiencing Harmony

1. Think of a successful person whom you know or know enough about. (Did you think of yourself? If not, why not? Would someone else think of you?) List ten qualities, attributes, and traits that you think make this person successful. Now think of a person who is living a life of significance. Make a second

list of the ten qualities, attributes, and traits that he or she possesses that make him or her significant. Are there any duplicate qualities that appear on both lists? What are they? Ask yourself if you have any of them. Could you acquire and develop them? (PS. If you're not clear how this exercise relates to harmony and our thinking about time, proceed onward to the next step!)

2. Choose one of the qualities, attributes, or traits that appeared on both lists and commit to amalgamating it into your everyday thoughts and behaviors for an entire day. Consciously use it to find more purpose in your job, more passion in your marriage, more imagination in raising your kids, and more creativity in serving your neighbors so that everybody helps everybody live significantly. The next day, choose another quality from your list and focus on making it part of the growing and developing you. Go through your list and repeat, if necessary, for thirty days in a row.

3. Analyze the two selected and admired individuals identified in Action Step 1 and try to figure out what matters most to them. Then make your own list of what matters most to you. Significant individuals always list any number of these: spouse, true love, spirituality, children, self-respect, education, occupational satisfaction, financial security (it is the "love of money," not money, that is the root of all evil), personal health and fitness, independence, quality of life, and inner peace.

4. Because harmony is a state of mind that we must constantly renew, small everyday reminders can help. Purchase a pack of

3x5 cards and make a small sign of each of the following sayings. Hang them up in three different visible locations in your
home to remind you that living your purpose every moment—
in other words, creating and experiencing harmony—is a
choice that only you can make and maintain.

- "Because your urge to continue is stronger than your desire
  to quit, and because there is a difference between temporary defeat and failure, when plans fail, you will substitute
  other plans but never change your purpose. You can always get more of what you want because you can always
  become more of who you are. No matter what your past
  has been you have a spotless future."
- "When we identify ourselves in terms of what we *do* instead
  of who we *are*, we become human *doings* instead of human
  beings—unacceptable if significance is what we seek."
- "Saying yes brings success. Saying no makes time and room
  for us to perfect and enjoy the art of significance."

Accept Others Instead of Judging Them

Acceptance is not excusing someone from the consequences of obedience. It is separating the person from the performance and loving him or her into obedience.

—SAMUEL W. CLARK, JR.

We've seen that significance is about obeying our consciences and the laws of a higher authority, persevering, stretching ourselves, trusting, learning the whole truth, cultivating a winning attitude, doing what's right, and living harmoniously. But our ability to become significant also depends on how we interpret others and their actions. To become significant, we must have the clarity and strength of will to nonjudgmentally accept others—and, for that matter, ourselves—for who and what they currently are. We are all different— biologically, culturally, ethnically, religiously, and as a result of our individual experiences in life. We also all grow and change at different paces. Successful people judge others on the basis of these differences. At best, they tolerate people who are unlike them in one respect or another; at worst, they regard differences as threatening. Significant people suspend judgments beyond a certain point, going beyond mere tolerance to attain and express true, deep, mindful acceptance of others and of themselves, just as they are.

Most of us understand that difference is the essence of humanity— that our unique characteristics should never be the source of hatred or conflict. Significant people reach the greatest heights because they have come, through soul searching and hard intellectual work, to *welcome and value* uniqueness and difference. Their cultivated stance of openness, grounded in a deep acceptance of their own authentic selves, allows them to stretch further, learn more, avoid the pitfalls of resentment and anger, and become the best they can be. It also enables them to stretch, inspire, teach, and lead others in a way that leaves a lasting legacy. We've seen that we have to meet people where they are in order to help them grow. As Carl Jung says "We cannot change anything until we accept it. . . . Once we accept our limits we go beyond them." As you read the stories in this chapter, I hope you will agree that accepting others and refraining from judging them lies at the very core of that emotional, spiritual, and physical state I've described as significance.

Mercy and Discipline

I am not, of course, suggesting that we suspend any and all judgments about people. That would be ridiculous. Even if we disavow the kinds of judgments implicit in prejudice and racism, as we most certainly must, there arises the issue of disciplining and punishing. In a society of laws, we still have to stand in judgment of the guilty so as to affirm what is right. But in this context, *how* we judge is critical—and illuminating. A conventional success mind-set requires strict justice, reasoning that when a law is broken, we must attach consequences or else the law has no meaning and we have no motivation to obey. The path to significance leads us to recognize that mere punishment is never enough; we must reach higher—to achieve empathy, acceptance, and, as we shall see in Law 12, "The Law of Forgiveness." Significant people don't simply abide by the letter of the law, but open their hearts and follow its *spirit*. They show *mercy*, defined as compassion or forgiveness extended to someone whom it is within one's power to punish or harm. Seneca said, "It is impossible to imagine anything which better becomes a ruler than mercy."

Mercy, rooted in an underlying acceptance, activates the emotional and spiritual parts of our being. As we become more significant, we become more willing to never give up on people, recognizing, as the old adage goes, that a broken clock is right twice a day, and that if we are not failing a few times, it means we are not pushing ourselves hard enough. Significant individuals don't close themselves off and merely tolerate the guilty; they know that because we enjoy free will, we all sometimes make bad choices, disappoint ourselves and others, and disobey a law here and there. Achieving significance means accepting even those who wrong us or let us down, and doing our best to create conditions for them to grow and reach their highest human potential.

Popular culture tends to celebrate the long arm of the law and its ability to detect and punish offenders. Characters like Dirty Harry or shows like *Law & Order* foment a misconception about discipline— that it's about punishing the guilty and giving them their due. No.

Without exception, discipline is to teach, not to punish, so the guilty are inspired to do better next time and improve their overall performance and awareness as human beings. This suggests that we refrain from an impulse to humiliate and chastise the guilty on account of their errant ways. You cannot increase a person's performance by making him feel worse. Humiliation immobilizes our behavior, contaminates our concentration, and dilutes our productivity. In a corporate environment, we cannot hope to lead by merely projecting our authority and striking fear in the hearts of our subordinates. Rudeness is a weak person's imitation of power. Remember, intimidation only works for a while, when the person feels fear. Once that person is no longer scared, he leaves. Gordon Hinckley said, "Hatred always fails and bitterness always destroys. Are there virtues more in need of application in our day, a time marked by litigious proceedings and heated exchanges, than those of forgiving, forgetting, and extending mercy to those who may have wronged us or let us down?"

How we discipline and punish ultimately ties back to how we see and treat ourselves. When we merely punish in strict accordance with the law, we hold offenders at arm's length, saying to ourselves, *"They* are different than *me."* We don't accept them, and at the core, that's because we also don't accept the parts of *ourselves* that misbehave and don't do as we should. We repress these parts, hide them, perpetuate the fiction that we are, in a sense, "perfect." By contrast, when we show mercy, we embrace even the seemingly uglier, less developed, less noble parts of humanity—and of ourselves. It's a higher path, ultimately even a divine one.

One of my most famous stories, written when I was thirteen, illustrates the point. My family and I are proud of this story and told it for many years until we published it on a holiday greeting card and then in my first book, back in 1983. It has subsequently appeared in the *Chicken Soup for the Soul* series, is an illustrated children's book, and was made into an award-winning film by Ron Krauss at Paramount Studios starring the late Jack Lemmon. It features a musical score by Academy Award winner Elmer Bernstein, and first aired at the Sundance Festival. It has won more than twenty-two film festival awards.

A storeowner was tacking a sign above his door that read PUPPIES FOR SALE. Signs like that have a way of attracting small children, and sure enough, a little boy appeared under the store's sign. "How much are you going to sell the puppies for?" he asked.

The storeowner replied, "Anywhere from $35 to $50."

The little boy reached into his pocket and pulled out some change. "I have $2.37," he said. "Can I please look at them?"

The storeowner smiled and whistled, and out of the kennel came Lady, who ran down the aisle of the store, followed by five teeny, tiny balls of fur. One puppy was limping, lagging considerably behind. Immediately the little boy singled out that puppy and asked, "What's wrong with that little dog?"

The storeowner explained that the veterinarian had examined the little puppy and had discovered that it didn't have a hip socket. It would always limp. It would always be lame. The little boy became excited. "That is the little puppy I want to buy."

The storeowner said, "No, you don't want to buy that little dog. If you really want him, I'll just give him to you."

The little boy got upset. He looked straight into the storeowner's eyes, pointed his finger, and said, "I don't want you to just give him to me. That little dog is worth every bit as much as all the other dogs, and I'll pay full price. In fact, I'll give you $2.37 now, and 50 cents a month until I have paid for him."

The storeowner countered, "You really don't want to buy this little dog. He is never going to be able to run and jump and play with you like the other puppies."

To this, the little boy reached down and rolled up his pant leg to reveal a badly twisted, crippled left leg supported by a big metal brace. He looked up at the storeowner and softly replied, "Well, I don't run so well myself, and the little puppy will need someone who understands!"

It's so vital that we accept the imperfect parts of ourselves first so that we can then extend that acceptance to those around us. Before we can fully accept others with their flaws, weaknesses, and limitations, before we can help them stretch from that place where they already are, we must commit to being the right person we know we should be. This automatically forces us to cut everyone some slack and unconditionally accept them for who they are, because we know how difficult it is for us to always do what's right.

Let's examine another way to look at this.

Authenticity

We must work to become *authentic* beings if we are to have any hope of practicing true, deep acceptance. Many writers have discussed authenticity, but, in brief, it means being real, being present in the moment, making ourselves open and vulnerable, and experiencing a life filled with self-discipline and self-love. Above all, authenticity entails active *self-acceptance*, demonstration of a willingness to own everything about us that makes us unique and special in the world, including our imperfections and limitations.

Authenticity allows us to serve as effective teachers and coaches, because the more authentic we are, the more we can set a powerful and positive example for others to follow. Our hearts become softer, and the more inclined we become to play with and hug our children who depend on us for their learning and growth. Whether in business or at home, significant individuals are authentic people who empathize, forgive, and teach rather than judge and punish. Most important, they encourage others to grow because they are currently and continuously growing themselves.

One reason authentic people don't judge others is because they understand growth's unpredictable, nonlinear nature. Many of us have growth trajectories like the famous growth cycle of the Chinese bamboo tree (described in Law 2, "The Law of Perseverance"): No sign of growth for the first eight years, then ninety-eight feet in four months. By not appreciating this larger picture, many of us short-circuit such growth, giving up in the first five years in many aspects of our lives, because we haven't achieved "best" status competing against others who seem to be growing and improving. And we disparage others as they grow, especially those at lower developmental levels than us, not realizing that tomorrow they're poised to grow ninety feet high! Do you now see why best is not all that it's cracked up to be? Do you perhaps wonder how being right—and *authentic*— is different?

"The Greatest"

Another important reason we should take care not to judge others who might occupy a lower developmental level than us is because as great and as accomplished as we may be, we still as human beings always remain works in process. I learned this lesson during a visit I was privileged to have with an American hero who fully understands the law of acceptance, boxing great Muhammad Ali. Born Cassius Marcellus Clay Jr. in Louisville, Kentucky, Ali grew up in a social and cultural environment that treated African Americans as second-class citizens. The city had segregated public facilities, and African Americans were the servants and poor working class; they could dream at most of becoming preachers or teachers at all-black churches and schools. But young Cassius dreamed bigger dreams. He knew he was somebody, refused to accept this destiny, and in his need to vent his frustration, discovered boxing.

Young Cassius had his first official boxing match at age twelve, winning by a split decision. Although he weighed only eighty-nine pounds, he jumped up and down, yelling, "I am the greatest. I will be the greatest fighter who ever lived." Years later, a childhood classmate remembered, "We were in elementary school together, and Cassius was just another one of the kids. You push and you shove each other, and you get into the normal fights. There were days he lost and days he won. So when he beat Sonny Liston to win the heavyweight championship, we all started laughing, saying, 'He's not even undefeated in the neighborhood. How can he be champion of the world?' "

Cassius Clay won the championship, converted to the Muslim faith, and changed his name to Muhammad Ali, yet because he did not accept induction into the U.S. Army on religious grounds, the authorities stripped him of his title. Years later, he was allowed to box again and won back the title two more times.

As a teenager, I had been a Golden Gloves boxer, and I took Ali as my idol. I emulated everything he did—from the tassels on my boots to the Ali Shuffle, the Rope-a-Dope, and the taunting jab. With fast hands and a desire to beat everybody, I was known as the "Great White Hope." Muhammad Ali truly was my hero, and I dreamed of meeting him.

In 1988 I had just finished speaking to the students of Andrews University in Berrien Springs, Michigan, when I discovered that Muhammad Ali lived there. Doctors had just diagnosed his Parkinson's disease, and the condition had not yet robbed him of his speech or dexterity. I asked the two gentlemen who were driving me around to grab a camera and take me to Ali's home. With my heart pounding, I took a deep breath and knocked on the front door. A woman answered and asked, "May I help you?"

I said, "Yes, ma'am. Is Muhammad in?"

"May I tell him who is calling?"

Sheepishly, I replied, "Sure, Dan Clark."

She walked away, and within seconds the imposing six-foot-three, 225-pound world champion filled the doorway. Muhammad smiled his famous smile and, in his quiet, breathy voice, invited me in. I asked if my friends could join us and whistled for them to come.

We sat in his living room for the next four and a half hours and watched videos of his greatest fights: the "Thrilla in Manilla," the "Rumble in the Jungle," and more. With his personal commentary, jokes, and stories, he made every move come alive. As the afternoon progressed, I took the opportunity to ask why a weaker, inferior opponent often knocks out a heavyweight champion. His answer was profound and obviously applies to business, education, and the military. He explained that when anyone starts defending his position—instead of playing to win, the competitor plays *not* to lose—he relinquishes the competitive advantage he had at the beginning of his career that allowed him to win the title in the first place. He reminded me that every sports champion, sales champion, and top-rated company needs to realize that *once the fight or competition begins, the champ no longer holds the title. He has put it up for grabs and must now fight to win it back.* Therefore, we should never accept complacency and always accept the reality that with hard work we can get better.

Ali then got right in my face and said, "Everybody knows I'm the greatest, but so are you! Do you believe it? You should. I do!"

All of us, even world champions, should remember that we can always be better, and that in this respect, we are no different from others at earlier developmental stages who are likewise questing to succeed. An awareness of this underlying similarity prevents us from judging anyone too harshly and prompts us to empathize, understand, and accept others as they are, so that they can continue to grow. The minute we start judging, viewing ourselves as superior, is the moment we cease being champions.

Olympic Magic

To inspire you to open your hearts, cultivate authenticity, and greet those who might be different in a spirit of understanding, I'd like to tell you about my experience carrying the Olympic torch on February

7, 2002, in Roy, Utah. General Motors sponsored the International Olympic Torch Relay, and the director of Special Projects at Chevy Trucks nominated me to be one of only 11,520 torchbearers world-wide to carry the torch over a route that began in Olympia, Greece, and covered 13,500 miles across 46 states (including on riverboats and in canoes) on a journey that took 65 days.

Each runner proudly ran holding the thirty-three-inch, three-and-a-half-pound butane-fueled torch, and each runner—among them cancer survivors, physically challenged, sick, dying, old, young—had a story. A high school student ran in front of his school wearing the shoes his brother had worn when he had been killed at that spot a week earlier. One man who ran on my day was a local firefighter whose father had lost his life as a firefighter at the World Trade Center on September 11, 2001. I was the final runner on day sixty-four, which meant that instead of carrying the torch the standard quarter mile, as most other runners did, I ran the last half mile and got to relight the cauldron mounted in the back of a special truck that transported the flame to downtown Salt Lake City for safe keeping until the next day's magnificent opening ceremonies.

Two weeks before I was to carry the torch, I received a white running suit fitted to my size with an accompanying letter explaining the Olympic flame's special significance. The letter boldly proclaimed that the flame had a soothing, mystical effect on world peace when it was put on display during the Olympic Games, but that the flame's transforming power was experienced and felt mostly by the torch runners themselves. The letter referred to us as "Keepers of the Flame."

During our orientation, we learned that when a torchbearer carries the flame, he and the flame become the single most significant symbol of world peace, hope, and goodwill at that single moment in time.

I was runner number ninety-two; runner number ninety-one was a serious, formal, yet delightful Chinese diplomat who headed the committee of the 2008 Olympic Games to be held in Beijing, China. Having a small 4-foot-11-inch Chinese Communist pass the flame to a 6-foot-5-inch blond, blue-eyed American Capitalist represented a wonderful moment in which we symbolically discarded our differences, came together as human beings to compete fairly, and created peace on earth. The power of the flame exposed cultural commonalities, which eliminate ridicule, prejudice, and anger, and remind us that we all belong to the human family.

My experience was phenomenal. As thousands of onlookers watched, cheered, chanted "U.S.A.," and waved miniature American flags, a police officer on the motorcycle escort turned on the gas container in my torch, and I stood in the middle of the road holding my torch out with both hands. The approaching torchbearer was instructed to stop, keep our torches eight inches apart, and let the flame leap from his torch to mine. The officer then extinguished his torch, and I ran off as the single keeper of the flame, representing everything the Olympic Games are about. This flame brought ninety-three countries together; ironically, people from ninety-three countries died in the World Trade Center terrorist attacks only a few months before.

Deeply moved by my experience, I interviewed the young lady onboard our shuttle bus who had been in charge of the entire sixty-five-day torch relay. I milked her for stories that proved true the power of the flame. With tears in her eyes, she told me of her responsibility as director of the relay to make sure every scheduled torchbearer showed up on time. If one canceled at the last minute, she would have to find a qualified replacement, orient him to the significance of being a keeper of the flame, fit him in the required white running suit, and take him to his relay segment.

When one man with cancer received his letter stating that he had been nominated to carry the torch, he immediately put the date on his calendar. Against his doctor's advice, he trained to be in shape when the day came. His cancer spread, and his training threw him into a coma. The lady in charge of the relay was notified, and while she was arranging a replacement runner, the man miraculously came out of his two-week coma on the morning of his run. An ambulance delivered him to the pick-up point. He was assisted to the middle of the road with his torch to receive the flame from the oncoming runner, had his torch ignited, and proudly ran his quarter-mile segment.

No one could believe it, and people cheered as they witnessed the inner strength exposed and supported by the spirit and power of the Olympic flame. As soon as the man lit the next runner's torch and his torch was extinguished, he collapsed in the road and was put back into the ambulance. Seconds later, he lapsed back into a coma and died soon after returning to the hospital.

When the torch relay came through Houston, Texas, one elderly woman phoned the night before her run to cancel. Early the next morning, the relay director drove along the relay route, prospecting for possibilities, when she happened upon an elementary school. She parked the bus, went inside, and asked to speak with the principal. With urgency in her voice, the relay director said she needed someone to carry the Olympic torch in about two hours and that the torchbearer would run directly in front of the school building. She asked the three people in the office—the principal, the counselor, and the secretary—if they could think of someone who could use the experience to help change the lives of others. Immediately they began spouting names of faculty; even the principal was nominated.

The relay director interrupted them and said, "I've changed my mind. I need the name of a young student who struggles at school with his grades, who is terribly lonely, whom other kids make fun of, who has been given up on by the teachers, who has a horrible home life, and who has low self-esteem."

All three fell silent and then at once blurted out the name of a fourth-grader, a scruffy, skinny, poor little ten-year-old boy. They called Billy to the office and informed him of his selection. They notified and invited his mother, who granted her permission. Billy was taken out to the bus, which had a closet full of running suits of every size, and directed on how to hold and carry his torch. Billy was also told about the importance of the Olympic movement and the special significance of carrying the torch—that he would be one of the most important people on earth for the time he was the Keeper of the Flame.

School was dismissed, small American flags were distributed, and faculty and students—unaware that Billy would be running—joined the thousands already lining the streets to cheer on the forthcoming torchbearers. As the shuttle bus drew closer, the crowd went wild. The torchbearer was running a quarter-mile behind, which allowed the bus to stop in time for the announcer to call the name of the new runner over the sound system, for the runner to be let off the bus, and for him to stand in the road and hold his torch out so that the approaching runner could ignite it.

Billy's name was announced, and the usually dirty kid emerged in his bright, clean, spectacular running suit holding the magnificent Olympic torch, which was almost as long as he was. Fellow students and faculty gasped, "What is this? Who let him do this? Did he steal the suit? Call the police and report an imposter! He must have stolen the torch!"

As Billy's predecessor ignited his torch and he started to run, somehow his name filtered through the crowd. Some people chanted, "Bill-y! Bill-y! Bill-y!" One by one, the skeptical, negative faculty members realized at that moment that little Billy was the world's ambassador of peace, that he alone epitomized the power of a positive dream. They couldn't help but join in with their support, chanting "Bill-y! Bill-y!" Fellow students couldn't hold back either as they, too, began to understand, shouting, "Go, Billy, go! Keep on truckin', Bro!" Billy's proud smile got so big and wide that he could have eaten a banana sideways!

Billy completed his quarter mile, lit the next torch, had his torch extinguished, and reboarded the bus to be taken back to a parking lot to meet his mom. The students and faculty returned to the school. Two days later, the relay director received an e-mail from the school's principal:

You have no idea what you have done for Billy, his family, and for me, our teachers, and students. None of us will ever be the same. The Olympic spirit and the power of that flame have helped us look for the good not the bad, to be positive, loving, forgiving, and definitely less judgmental. We have been reminded that every kid matters and now understand the deepest meaning of "Leave no child behind." Thank you, thank you! PS—Billy no longer sits alone!

Mentoring

It's amazing how quickly we transform from successful to significant when we open our hearts, accept others, and extend mercy rather than merely judge. That many educators unfortunately don't know this became crystal clear one morning at a middle school in Georgetown, Texas, when the principal called a surprise mandatory faculty meeting. One hundred adult influencers, including teachers, counselors, cafeteria personnel, bus drivers, custodians, and secretaries assembled on one side of the multipurpose room. On the other side, the principal had the names of each of his six hundred students printed on individual cards and hung on the wall. His directions were simple. He gave each of the attendees ten adhesive gold stars and asked them to walk across the room and place a star by the name of a student he or she had a relationship with. They returned to their seats and the principal had the numbers tabulated. Moments later he sadly reported what he had suspected. With tears in his eyes he said, "Twenty-five percent of the students had ten or more stars by their name. Another twenty-five percent of the students had five stars by their name. And fifty percent of these precious young men and women had no stars at all!"

We must stop judging and start treating others of all ages and interests exactly as we ourselves want to be treated—reaching out to help everyone in our charge to feel wanted, important, loved, and capable. I learned this from a young man in a northern Utah high school who participated in a unique directive that integrated students with a physical or mental challenge into mainstream classes.

To make the directive work, the administration organized a mentor program that teamed one special-needs student with a mainstream student who would help and mentor. The school athletic director presented the idea to the captain of the football team. John was a tall, strong, intense young man—not the patient, caring type needed for this kind of program. He made it clear that this wasn't "his thing" and he didn't have time to be a mentor. But the athletic director knew it would be good for John and insisted he volunteer.

John was matched with Randy, a young man with Down syndrome. Reluctant and irritated at first, John tried to lose Randy, but very soon John got used to him and welcomed the constant company. Randy not only attended every one of John's classes and ate with him at lunchtime, but he also came to football practice with him. After a few days, John asked the coach to make Randy the official team manager, responsible for the balls, tape, and water bottles. At the end of the football season, the team won the state championship, and John was named state MVP. Randy was presented with a school letterman's jacket. The team cheered as Randy put it on. It was the coolest thing that had ever happened to him. From that day forward, Randy never took it off. He slept in his jacket and wore it throughout each weekend.

Basketball season started, and John became the captain and star of the team. At John's request, the team again named Randy manager.

During the basketball season, John and Randy remained inseparable. Not only did John take Randy to special occasions—like dances as a joint escort for his girlfriend—but he also took Randy to the library to tutor him in his classes. John himself became a much better student as he tutored Randy, and John made the honor roll for the first time in more than a year. The mentor program had made that school year the most rewarding year of John's life.

Then tragedy struck in the middle of the state basketball tournament. Randy fell ill and died of pneumonia. The funeral took place the day before the championship game. John addressed the mourners, sharing his deep, abiding friendship and respect for Randy. He told how Randy had taught him about real courage, self-esteem, love, and the importance of giving 100 percent in everything he did. John dedicated the upcoming state finals game to Randy and concluded his remarks by stating that he was honored to have received the MVP award in football and the leadership plaque for being the captain of the basketball team. "But," John added, "the real leader of both the football and basketball teams was Randy, for he accomplished more with what he had than anyone I've ever met. Randy inspired all who knew him."

John walked from behind the podium, took off the irreplaceable state football MVP medallion that hung around his neck, leaned into the open casket, and placed it on Randy's chest. Then he placed his leadership plaque next to it. Randy was buried in his letter jacket, surrounded by John's cherished awards as well as pictures and letters left by those who admired him. The next day, John's team won the championship and presented the game ball to Randy's family. John went to college on a full athletic scholarship, eventually earning a master's degree in education. Today John is a special-education teacher and volunteers ten hours a week for the Special Olympics. (When the state athletic association heard what John had done, it presented him with another MVP medallion that had been made especially for him.)

The Bottom Line

What we've been in the past does not make us who we are today; what we hope to become in the future does. Successful people judge others. They impose justice, merely tolerate differences, and satisfy themselves with strict adherence to the letter of the law. They stay within the realm of the rational and the logical. Significant individuals live the advanced, higher Law of Acceptance, serving as a beacon and inspiration for others to do the same. Let us strive for total acceptance, first of ourselves, and then of all other human beings with "pre-existing conditions"—of height, weight, physical or mental disabilities, race, color, creed, education, school performance, financial status, health habits, gender, sexual orientation, and lifestyle. Let us give up the stigmas we place on one another and cleanse our consciences so that we all can continue to grow into whole, fulfilled, authentic people.

Four Suggested Action Steps to Learning Acceptance

1. Visit a homeless shelter and/or soup kitchen in your area and volunteer to serve those in need. By hearing the stories of the

underserved, you will begin to learn to accept the unfortunate instead of judging them.

2. Psychologists regard the receiving of attention as the number one motivator of human performance. If we can't get attention for doing something positive, we will get attention for doing something negative. Therefore, don't hold negative behavior against someone. If you discipline yourself to catch others doing something right and to reinforce the behaviors you want repeated, eventually their behavior will improve and meet the organization's standards. Begin with only one person, and continue one person, one moment at a time.

3. For one full day, and then one full week, refuse to honk your horn at another driver for doing something stupid (obviously we all have done what he or she just did!); refuse to yell at anyone at home or at work who angers or disappoints you; and refuse to walk by an indigent homeless person without giving him or her a dollar with an encouraging word. Then continue this—for the rest of your life!

4. Write one note a day to a family member, a neighbor, and a coworker (that's three total notes per day) that simply thanks them for who they are, for their example and friendship, and for what they do that makes you a better person. Start with familiar relationships, but then reach out to those who are different than you, whom you still admire and respect. We cannot reread a telephone conversation, and a text or an e-mail is too impersonal. A note in your handwriting is a precious gift they will never throw away!

Love and Be Needed Instead of
Romanced and Used

The individual's most vital need is to prove his worth, and this usu-
ally means an insatiable hunger for action wherein he develops and
employs his capacities and talents through love, admiration, and
genuine interest in the life of another.

—ERIC HOFFER

There is romance, and there is love. What's the difference? If I love
you because you are beautiful, that's romance. If you are beautiful
because I love you, that's real love—a value creating love that inspires
us to become everything we were born to be. However, we can be
liked and feel loved, but unless we know we are truly needed, we will
never fulfill the full measure of our existence and enjoy the realm of
significance.

Mere romance, which successful people cultivate, is an emotional
attachment built around ego and selfishness, a virtual obsession to
take more than you give. Obviously romance is an enjoyable thing

we all seek, but unaccompanied by love, it can quickly become destructive. In fact, romance is often little more than a politically correct label for lust, an ugly, conditional relationship rooted in excessive self-importance and boastful arrogance.

Significant individuals learn to rise above romantic selfishness to achieve love, with all its intensity, power, turbulence, frustration, yearning, attraction, restraint, forbidding, peace, beauty, and sublimity. True love is unselfish and involves giving more than you get. It represents unconditional cherishing and concern for another, a fulfillment of the other's needs that also brings about the attendant and sublime pleasure of being needed. Our chances of living the Twelve Laws of Significance rise to 100 percent probability when we have someone by our side who truly loves us, who is easing the burden, and whom we love in turn.

Love's Universal Relevance

We may question the need for love in our professional lives, but from a productivity perspective, peak performance is always about love. If our performance is fueled by ego-driven competition, whether in sales, marketing, customer service, or football, basketball, baseball, soccer, or golf, our efforts devolve into a task of keeping score and beating the other person or team, which results in stress, anxiety, pressure, and a crisis when we fall behind. However, if we sell, grow market share and awareness, resolve customer complaints, or serve in the military for the pure love of the endeavor, out of a desire to give of ourselves and fulfill others' needs, we easily and naturally achieve superior results.

When I speak to athletic teams right before their championship games, I remind them that they aren't competing against or defeating their opponent. They are playing only for the love of the game. They make an amazing pass, cleverly dribble past who's guarding them, shoot a clutch shot, leap high to head a corner kick into the net, hit a game-winning home run, score a last-second touchdown, and sink a long putt, simply because they can—simply because they loved to practice, and today is the day for them to realize the fruits of their efforts. They play out-of-their-heads because they love giving themselves over to the game, and they love who they are in the process.

In the world of dance competition, if a dancer focuses only on scoring the highest point total and on beating his or her competitors, she experiences stress and pressure accompanied by a muscle tenseness that results in mechanically marking the steps to the music. However, if the dancer competes simply because she loves to dance and looks at it as nothing more than another opportunity to give a gift back to the world (by showcasing her talent with passion, imagination, and creativity), she feels no stress, understands that pressure is not naturally present, and finds her flow. A distinct and measureable difference exists between *doing* the choreography and *being* the choreography—between merely making the movements and performing the dance.

Perhaps the most comprehensive statement I know of love's universal applicability comes from Dieter Uchtdorf, who explains,

> Love ought to be at the center of everything we do in our own family, in our charitable giving, and in our livelihood. Love is the healing balm that repairs rifts in personal and family

relationships. It is the bond that unites families, communities, and nations. Love is the power that initiates friendship, tolerance, civility, and respect. It is the source that overcomes divisiveness and hate. Love is the fire that warms our lives with unparalleled joy and divine hope. Love should be our walk and our talk. When we truly understand what it means to love, any confusion we have about life and our unique place in it clears and our priorities align. Our walk through the halls of life becomes more joyful. Our lives take on new meaning. Our relationships become more profound. Obedience becomes a joy rather than a burden. Love allows us to look beyond our physical attributes and see and appreciate the inner qualities and traits that don't diminish with time.

Defining Real Love

I have contrasted the highest law of love with the preparatory principle of romantic selfishness, but that does not suffice to convey what love truly is. In a philosophical context, love is a virtue representing all of human kindness, compassion, and affection. In a religious context, love is not just a virtue, but the basis for all being (God is love). The word "love" can refer to a variety of different feelings, states, and attitudes, ranging from generic pleasure ("I loved that meal") to intense devotion ("I love my wife") to the emotional closeness of familial love ("I love my children") to the platonic love that defines friendship—even to the reality that dogs never lie about love (like my Maltese Porsha, who is always excited to see me, regardless of how late I come home, if I gain weight, or lose my job).

This diversity of uses and meanings, combined with the complexity of the feelings involved, makes love unusually difficult to define consistently, even compared with other emotional states. When I talk of love, I don't mean the puppy love of elementary years, and definitely not the confused love of teenagers, but the full-blown love of eligible and mature men and women—love, in other words, as a commitment. True love is the ultimate expression of altruism, the all-giving, selfless concern for another's well-being. It's a fortunate wife who has a husband willing to give his life for her, and a husband who has a wife worthy of such a sacrifice is just as blessed. Usually such sacrifices are made for the sake of growth. As M. Scott Peck said, love is "the will to extend one's self for the purpose of nurturing one's own or another's spiritual growth and happiness." We grow because we're working at it, and we're working at it because we love ourselves. In turn, our love of others leads us to assist them in loving themselves so that they can love another, and love's evolution continues.

True love means you love the whole person, complete with all of that individual's flaws, idiosyncrasies, and quirks. We most often reveal true love when we express heartfelt appreciation for our beloved *without* making love, while snuggling in each other's arms. When we experience true love, we celebrate a special, uncommon, deep connection born out of admiration, respect, and selflessness. True love endures, whereas lust changes as quickly as we can flash an erotic image in our minds, turn a pornographic page, or glance at yet another potential object for gratification.

Love is when you're away from your loved one and think, *I like me best when I'm with you. I want to see you again and again and be with you forever.* Love elevates, protects, respects, enriches, and motivates us to sacrifice for each other. As a process, love takes time and requires personal action. Too often we mistake expediency—adherence to self-serving infatuation, stimulation, persuasion, and lust—for love. Many even regard love as mere physical attraction, when, in reality, physical gratification is only incidental to love. We cannot measure real love in terms of moonlight and roses, but in terms of who will care for us when we grow old.

Unlike mere romance, true love is realizing that you have to be a friend before you can be a lover, and that you love your friend not because he or she is perfect, but because he or she is perfect for *you*. Make no mistake: I am not suggesting that a soul mate wanders the earth waiting for you. This myth, rooted in ancient Greek mythology, and epitomizing self-centered, narcissistic thinking, is a major destroyer of relationships. As presented in Plato's *Symposium*, the myth holds that humans had four arms, four legs, and a single head made of two faces. Because Zeus feared their power, he split them all in half, resulting in a perpetual ache of separation and a longing to regain the completeness by finding one's missing half to re-create the whole. Although harmless terms like "my better half" and "counterpart" evolved from this thinking, another human being was not created just to satisfy your needs or my needs, just to make us feel complete. Yet many believe and pray that destiny will lead them to the "right one," freeing them from having to do the hard and honest work of selecting a mate. When our relationships fail, we attribute it to not having found our Mr. or Ms. Right. Then we cut our losses, get divorced, and return to our hapless quest for the one who, once found, will cause us to live happily ever after.

For this reason, when it comes to relationships, love is not the answer—it's the assignment! And based on this comprehensive understanding, romance is only the preparatory law for the advanced, highest Law of Loving and Being Needed.

Being Needed

Significant individuals know what it means to be genuinely needed. To illustrate, let me take you back to the 1980s when I was the main professional speaker in President Ronald Reagan's White House who took First Lady Nancy Reagan's "Just Say No" positive-choices school program nationwide. While speaking to hundreds of thousands of teenagers in hundreds of high schools in all fifty states, I became deeply involved in the suicide epidemic that was sweeping across North America. Plano, Texas, saw six suicides in the same day—seven in the same week. I conducted special programs to help communities deal with suicides in New Jersey, Utah, South Dakota, California, Florida, New York, Vermont, Massachusetts, and Connecticut.

In Iowa, one hundred suicide attempts took place within thirty days at the same high school. One girl died. The school brought in Charlotte Ross, a national consultant on suicide, and me to talk to kids and families. We gathered with counselors, school administrators, and health-care professionals to interview each of the students who had attempted suicide. To our surprise, they all told us that they wanted to give up on themselves and on life because they lacked commitment relationships. We have already established that love is a commitment. However, "I love you" are not the world's three most powerful, commitment-oriented relationship words. The three most powerful words are "I need you." These kids told us they knew they were liked, they knew they were loved, but they didn't believe they were needed. And when we don't feel that we are needed, why hang around?

One of my friends decided to get married. He asked if I would write a song and sing it at his wedding. I said no. He proceeded to remind me that we were best friends and that it would be cool for me to participate in his special day. He basically made me feel important. Everyone likes to feel important.

I finally gave in and wrote the song. Two days later, he phoned back to explain that the band had just canceled, and he wanted me to prepare forty to fifty songs to play as the dinner entertainment. I emphatically said, "No way!" He said, "I need you." Had he said, "I love you," I would have responded, "I love you too—here is the number of a band." But "I need you" made me feel that I was not just good, but that I was good for something—that I really mattered, that I could make a significant contribution. I couldn't turn him down, and I don't think you could have, either.

When my friend's wedding day arrived, I sang the song that I had written for the couple. But before I could sing another tune, the band arrived. There was a miscommunication. I didn't want to sing all night, anyway. I wanted to eat and socialize like everybody else, so I helped the band members set up their equipment. Now, think about this: When I arrived at the wedding reception, I arrived with the attitude that my friend needed me. I would have stayed until four o'clock in the morning if necessary, because he needed me. I would have waited tables, mopped the floor, and contributed in any way I could, because he needed me. But the second the band showed up, I was no longer needed. We can fool others, but we can't fool ourselves. So I left the reception and went home.

Are you needed? If not, why not? And what are you going to do about it right now? In the corporate arena, when a sales champion or outstanding executive jumps ship to work for the competition, it is not always about money. There's a good chance that person no longer feels needed where he is, so he goes where he does feel needed. Most of us think outside attention and recognition motivate us. It doesn't, yet we emphasize it in our marriages, personal relationships, business contracts, and athletic endeavors. What we desperately desire is to be genuinely needed.

In contemporary American society, we can't afford to wait for someone to tell us or show us that we are needed. It may never happen. We could go for months before we experience this crucial validation. So what do we do—give up, quit, kill ourselves? Most definitely not. Whom are we fooling to think that society has to give our lives meaning, purpose, and excitement? *We* bear responsibility to do something on a daily basis to prove to ourselves that we are needed. If you don't feel needed at work, participate more, volunteer, and get involved on committees and event-planning boards. If you don't feel needed at home, participate more, get involved. If you don't feel needed by your children, participate more, get involved in their world, volunteer in their schools, host their parties at your home, stay in touch, get involved in their friends' lives. If you don't feel needed in your neighborhood or world, vote, participate in charity organizations, give more than you take, and leave everything and everyone in better shape than you found them.

The glory of love is not companionship, but rather the spirited inspiration that comes when we discover that someone else believes in us and is willing to trust us. Love is knowing that I don't love you because I need you (this is codependence); I need you because I love you, and I need you to need me, too (this is interdependence). To illustrate the notion of love as the experience of being needed, I offer another story about a death—not just any death, one that really hit home for me. As I mentioned in Law 3, my dear, sweet dad battled cancer for six and a half years. As the pain mounted and Dad's last day was approaching, I hoped I could be by his bedside when he took his last breath. That didn't happen for me. I had to fly out to Seattle, Washington, to give two speeches to two large groups—one at a conference on Friday morning, the other on Saturday.

I was staying at the Seattle Airport Marriott Hotel. It was early Friday morning, October 12. I had shaved and showered and put on my coat and tie when the phone rang. Thinking it was my ride to the convention center, I picked up the phone and almost flippantly said, "I'll be right there." Fifteen seconds of silence later, my younger brother's voice came through, "Dad passed away this morning at seven a.m."

I sat down on the bed, the tears flowing down my cheeks. "How is Mom?"

"Good."

"Give her a big hug and a kiss for me, and tell her I'll phone her in a little while."

Paul then asked me the gazillion-dollar question, "What are you going to do?"

After thinking it over, I said, "I'm going to go make my speech.

That's what Dad would want me to do. He always taught us to only make commitments that we can keep and to always keep those commitments." I couldn't imagine being the meeting planner with more than thirty-five hundred people sitting in the audience and not have the speaker show up. I told my brother that I needed to stay and speak, spend the night, speak the next day, and then hustle home.

I hung up and broke down, crying like a baby. My dad, my hero, was gone. I felt wrenched with regrets. Every thought and word was, *"I wish I . . . If only I had . . ."* Yes, I've done a lot of pretty cool things in my life and have had an exciting time. But I would trade all of it for one more day with my dad. When I interview older people, I am often told that they do not have regrets for things they did; they have regrets only for the things they did not do. I know what they mean.

The phone rang again. This time it was my ride. I told him I would be right down. I went into the washroom, splashed water onto my face, left my room, and stepped into the elevator. As the elevator doors closed, the corner of a bellman's cart crammed its way through the narrow opening and the doors reopened. On the elevator came an overzealous, way-too-cheery bellman. He pushed his cart to the middle, forcing me back to the rear corner. Trying to avoid eye contact, I stood with my head down, hands clasped in the "elevator position." As the doors closed, he blurted, "Whoa! Did you see the beautiful sunshine today? I've lived here in Seattle all of my eighteen years, and it's rained every single day. You must have brought the happy weather with you. How ya doin'?"

Not looking up, I said, "Fine."

He kept staring at me until he again blurted, "No, sir, you're not fine. Your eyes are red and a little puffy. You've been crying."

"Yeah. I just found out that my dad died this morning, and I'm really sad."

"Whoa," the bellman said. He went quiet until the doors opened at the lobby. He went left and I went right.

I had to dig deeper that night than I had ever dug to rise to the occasion, but I did, and I made my speech. At the end of my speech, I told the audience I would conclude with a song from one of my albums. I told them I was singing it because my dad had died that morning, and it would be the first time he had ever heard me sing it in public.

I finished the song and had the driver take me back to the Seattle Airport Marriott Hotel. When I walked into the hotel room, I found a basket of fruit resting on the chest of drawers. Not your basic basket delivered from the hotel gift shop with the colored cellophane cover, ribbon bow, and small sterile stamped card from the manager that seldom gets your name right—*Thanks for staying with us, Ralphie*. This was a broken basket, slightly smashed on one side. It appeared as if it was a last-minute gesture executed with limited resources. Whoever delivered it was obviously into presentation because the crinkled portion of the basket was turned toward the wall and covered by a big rubberized leaf that had apparently been picked off the fake tree in the lobby. In the basket, I found two oranges, an apple, a big ripe tomato, and a huge carrot.

Most important, I found a handwritten note that read: "Mr. Clark, I'm sure sorry your dad died. I was off work today at 5 p.m., but I came back tonight so I could be here for you. Room service closes at 10 p.m., but the kitchen has decided to stay open all night long so they can be here just for you. If you need anything, just call and ask for me." It was signed, "James—the bellman in the elevator." James was not the only one to sign the card: Every employee that night at the Seattle Airport Marriott Hotel did. I have it framed and hanging in my office.

Here we have James, an eighteen-year-old young man, the youngest and lowest-paid person on the entire employee payroll, who "gets" three things: First, you can't pay enough for experience. (And PS: Age has nothing to do with success or significance. How do we know? Some of the greatest songs you'll ever hear were written by young men and women. Why? Because they have access to the same twelve notes the old folks do.) Second, James realizes money isn't a motivator; exceeding expectations is. He clearly understands that we are not paid by the hour, but for the value we bring to that hour. Third, James understands the self-discipline and integrity—the character, the *obedience*—it takes to create loyal customers. Every time I speak, I stay at the posh hotel where my clients are holding the meeting. However, because of James, whenever I speak in Seattle, Washington, I always stay at the Airport Marriott Hotel, even if I have to rent a car at my own expense and drive two hours out of my way to get there.

What it's really all about is unconditionally loving and giving more than we take so that we prove to ourselves that we are truly needed. We can do this in our personal lives, but we can also do this at work, with customers and bosses alike, with everyone we meet. Unconditionally loving and giving—not because they have to, but because they expect it of themselves—is what James and his colleagues did so well that night.

The Bottom Line

Successful people settle for the preparatory principle of selfish romance. Significant individuals live the advanced, highest Law of Love. Love is universally relevant, expressed in contexts as diverse as married life, everyday work, and athletics. To love is to give unselfishly of ourselves, fulfilling others' needs, and in the process proving to ourselves that we are needed. No, significant people are not in codependent relationships, in which the parties need the other in order to survive. Rather, they are in interdependent relationships, in which the parties need the others to *thrive*. Mere romance can devolve into lust, but love brings out the highest, noblest parts of our being, enabling us to experience life to the fullest and to realize our purpose as humans. All of us, even the humblest bellman, can show loving concern for another's well-being, inspiring others to cultivate altruistic, loving relationships in turn.

Four Suggested Action Steps to Loving and Being Needed

1. List the ten people you love most, explaining in a sentence or two why you love them. Evaluate the difference in the kind of love and level of intensity with which you love each of them— is your love based on romance or true love? Do you love them because of what they give you, or do you love them generously and selflessly, pouring yourself out for them?
2. List one need of each of the people you listed in action step one. Plan a concrete action you can take to help meet each of those needs.

3. List the five actions that others do for you that make you feel most loved. Thank those who do those actions for you and let them know that they are needed.

4. List the five places (destinations) and five things (car, boat, vacation home, sport, hobby, etc.) that you love most. Compare the amount of time, money, and energy that you spend on these things to the time, money, and energy you spend on the people you listed earlier. If you are putting more into your own selfish pursuits than into your relationships, consider how to change your priorities.

Establish Covenants Instead of
Making Commitments

And it is the Soldier, who salutes the flag,
Who serves beneath the flag,
And whose coffin is draped by the flag,
Who allows the protester to burn the flag.

—ATTRIBUTED TO CHARLES MICHAEL PROVINCE, U.S. ARMY

Upon his very first entrance into the House of Commons as Britain's new prime minister on May 13, 1940, Winston Churchill received only a lukewarm reception from the assembly while outgoing Prime Minister Neville Chamberlain was heartily cheered. But Churchill refused to be swayed by what others thought or said and made the first of his many morale-boosting speeches.

As Hitler's armies were storming across Europe, seemingly unstoppable, and when the survival of Great Britain itself appeared rather uncertain, Churchill was defiant and determined. No matter how he was treated by his fellow countrymen, he offered his "blood, toil, tears and sweat" in order to attain "victory, however long and hard the road may be."

With those words, he moved beyond a commitment to his nation to a covenant—he would serve his nation out of love no matter what.

Webster defines "commitment" as: "an agreement or pledge to do something in the future . . . the state or an instance of being obligated or emotionally impelled." A commitment is a two-way contract between two or more parties predicated on performance, born out of suspicion, and usually bound by a written agreement of requirements. Sadly, requirements usually represent a minimum standard in relationships. In a commitment contract, the parties do not trust each other, and they consequently set limits to their own responsibility with a document of "if you do this, I will do that." Accountability is important, but a commitment contract bears no feeling, emotional attachment, or moral obligation to perform.

We can define "covenant," the higher law realized by significant individuals, as a solemn binding promise to do something in the present now. A covenant is a one-way promise between two or more parties, predicated on principles and bound by sacrifice—an unwritten conviction that "I will do this *regardless* if you do that." Max De Pree, retired CEO of Herman Miller, speaks of a covenant between an organization and an individual in contrast to the traditional contractual commitment (i.e., an honest day's pay in exchange for an honest day's work): "Contracts are a small part of a relationship. A complete relationship needs a covenant relationship, which rests on a shared commitment to core values, to ideas, to issues, and to goals."

To transcend success and walk the path toward significance, we must forge as many covenant relationships as possible, paying attention to the burning spirit behind our connections rather than limit ourselves to a strict, pragmatic, egocentric, letter-of-the-law notion of our own responsibilities. Let us embrace *covenant service*, defined as an act of trading something valued for the sake of something else regarded as more important or worthy. It's the baseball batter willingly bunting the ball that puts himself out but allows his teammate to advance as the base runner; it is trading sleep for finishing the task, and days off work for finishing the job on time; it is giving something more than is required. As significant individuals know, as any real winners in life know, making a covenant to live the principles of integrity, virtue, and fidelity sustains a much higher standard of performance than signing the dotted line on a physical contract. And, ultimately, we are the ones who benefit most from this enhanced responsibility and performance.

Varieties of Covenant Bonds

Covenant bonds can operate in all kinds of relationships, among all kinds of people. I once rode in a car with my friend, the former three-time World Professional Wrestling Champion Diamond Dallas Page. His phone rang, and it was an old acquaintance from New Jersey who had taken advantage of him in business and who was calling to ask Dallas if he would hook him up with great seats and backstage passes to his buddy Bruce Springsteen's concert. Dallas said yes, asked about the caller's family, and told him whom to call and what to do. When he hung up, Dallas's wife, Kimberly, scolded him, "Why are you always so nice to everyone? All this guy ever does is use you."

Dallas smiled and calmly replied, "Why should I allow what someone else says or does change who I am or my desire to do the right thing?"

Strong marriages, too, are by nature covenants, not just private contracts one may cancel at will. We can remember this by comparing the shepherd with the hireling. A hireling works on a temporary basis, bound only by a contract; when he sees the wolves, he doesn't care about the sheep, and he runs. A shepherd knows each sheep by name, and they know his voice, and because his relationship is unconditionally based on love, he is willing to risk his life for his sheep. Likewise, in marriages, the deepest, most meaningful love arises out of a one-way covenant service, where you concern yourself with serving the other before yourself and with giving everything to your partner without expecting anything in return. This in turn allows you to prove to yourself that you are needed, which makes the ultimate application of covenant service, love.

Of course, all relationships involve two (or more) people, and you control only one of them. You can't change anyone but yourself. Therefore, when it comes to covenant service, we love and serve others *in spite of* their actions, rather than because of them.

Covenant also operates on a communal level, in the related concept of *consecration*. Consecration entails the mind-set of "all for one and one for all"—when the water in the lake goes up, all the boats rise together. It's a pledge to dedicate our time, talents, and material resources to the building up of others for everyone's benefit. Such a pledge reflects, at the core, a realization that we all die, and no matter how much stuff we accumulate, we can't take it with us; we are merely "renting" a portion of the earth's natural resources and using them while we pass through this mortal existence. It's not your ocean, my air, your land, my drinking water, your atmosphere. Under a service-before-self, covenant-to-consecration orientation, we behave industriously and avoid idleness, overcome personal pride and greed, improve our talents for the good of all, seek the interest of our neighbors, develop a greater sense of charity, and eliminate poverty from the face of the earth. Covenant service is about unconditionally loving all humans, not because of something they did or who they are, but because of who we all are!

Climbing Rocky Ridge

Once we make covenant service an automatic attitude and response, we can comprehend the long-term ramifications commonly referred to as *legacy*. To many, leaving a legacy involves opening your pockets and donating millions to a university to have a building named after you. To me, it entails giving of ourselves from the heart. I learned about the covenant bond and legacy setting when I participated in a reenactment of the 1856 western migration of pioneers along the Oregon-Mormon Trail. From July 17 to 20, 2006, our group of 380 men, women, and teenagers picked up the historic trail on the plains of Wyoming at a place called Martin's Cove. It was here that the Martin Handcart Company sought shelter from a brutal storm in the fall of 1856. They had already pulled their five-hundred-pound hand-carts from Omaha, Nebraska, and had worn out their shoes, some folks walking barefoot. Many died from exposure and were buried in shallow graves along the way.

With five to eight people assigned to each of our carts, our group left this special place pulling three-hundred-pound handcarts on a forty-one-mile, three-day trek that culminated in a five-and-a-half-mile climb over a steep, treacherous, bumpy stretch called Rocky Ridge, named because of the countless jagged, sometimes large, and often slippery rocks poking out of the rutted ground. At just over seven thousand feet, Rocky Ridge was one of the highest peaks on the more than thirteen hundred total miles of the trail. It took us four hours to pull and push our handcarts up and over the mountain and out to Rock Creek Camp. We arrived at a small cemetery and discovered thirteen gravestones honoring those who had passed away at this location along the trail. At an evening memorial service, I heard an incredible story about a young man named James Kirkwood.

James and his family came from Scotland and had to save for a long time for passage to America. James's father got sick and died shortly after they arrived, but his mother was determined to fulfill her husband's dream and go on to the Salt Lake Valley. James was eleven years old and had three brothers: Thomas, nineteen, was physically challenged with a crippled leg and had to ride in the hand-cart; Robert, twenty-one, helped their mother pull the cart; and Joseph, four, traveled under James's care.

On October 20, 1856, the handcart company camped by the Sweetwater River, not far from the base of Rocky Ridge. Having had little to eat for several days, everyone felt weak and cold. Ahead lay a long, steep climb through snow drifting as high as the axles on the handcarts. With freezing wind blowing in their faces and through their clothes, these pioneers traveled all day and all night.

Young Joseph's shoes had worn out from walking the previous thousand-plus miles, and his little feet were numb. Joseph fell down and started to cry. James tried to encourage him to climb some more, but Joseph couldn't take another step. James picked him up and began to climb the ridge. Joseph was heavy, and James had to move slowly, carrying his little brother on his shoulder, then in his arms, then over his other shoulder. The two boys fell behind the main group, but James never gave up. Sometimes Joseph would start to slip because James's fingers were frozen and he couldn't hold on very well. James would set Joseph down, rest for a moment, pick him up again, and continue walking.

After taking more than twenty-seven hours to get up and over Rocky Ridge, James saw the fires burning at Rock Creek Camp. The boys had made it to safety. James had been quiet for a long time, and young, thankful Joseph couldn't get him to talk. James dragged his little brother over to the rest of the group and set him down by the fire before collapsing, never to rise again. Having given everything he had, eleven-year-old James Kirkwood lay down and died.

Yes, covenant entails service to a cause greater than ourselves and to each other, and it results in legacies lasting decades, even generations. Since my own trek experience, I often wonder if I could or would have laid my life down for a loved one or a friend. Would you have? How far would you go to serve a customer or a teammate? How far would you go to save a spouse? The answers you present to questions like these can give you some sense of how far down the path to significance you have already traveled, and the kind of message you are sending to your children and grandchildren.

A Call for More Covenant Service

James Kirkwood's story is an American story, and it serves as a potent reminder that covenant relationships have made America what she is today. Have you noticed a decline lately, or is it just me?

I fly on Delta Airlines and hold their highest Diamond Medallion status, which means I have access to their customer-service hotline, called Special Member Services. One day in 2012, my flight into Washington, D.C.'s Reagan National Airport was canceled. When I phoned the special number for emergency VIP help, a polite, professional woman greeted me by name and asked how she could help me. I explained my crisis and what I needed her to do. She said, "I'm sorry, Mr. Clark, I can't do that."

In the past, I would have used my persuasive skills to explain that she shouldn't allow "can't" to mean "won't," and that her refusal to help me was a choice she didn't have to make. Where there's a will, there is always a *won't*, but there's always a way—she just needed to find it. But not once have I ever succeeded in getting a customer-service agent to change his or her mind, so I didn't waste my time. Instead, I asked her which call center she was working at, and she told me Cincinnati. I thanked her, hung up the telephone, and immediately called back the same special number. A different woman answered, politely and professionally greeted me by name, and asked the same question: "How may I help you?" I explained my exact same crisis and made the same request. She said, "No problem, Mr. Clark. I can do that."

Both customer-service agents had undergone the same training and had access to the same software solutions. One said no, one said yes. One was complacent and took her job for granted; the other appreciated her employment, took pride in her career, and in some measure viewed her relationship with customers as a one-way, covenant kind of arrangement. I was in a huge hurry, but I asked this second customer-service agent to tell me her location. With a beautiful, barely noticeable accent, she replied, "India."

We must regain a sense of covenant service in our business dealings, both individually and organizationally. Certainly as customers we expect a higher level of service before self from the organizations with which we do business. According to a five-year Cone/Roper study, Americans still value highly overall corporate responsibility and citizenship. More than 60 percent of consumers will switch retailers if they support the same cause the consumer supports while nine in ten workers feel a greater sense of pride and a stronger sense of loyalty to their companies because of cause-marketing programs, translating into enhanced customer service and positive word of mouth.

Beyond the business world, our brave airmen, sailors, Marines, and soldiers remain the premier example of covenant service before self. They are always giving something more—often all they have. For this reason, I hope you will step up your support for our troops and their amazing families. I know I have. On one occasion, I was sitting in my first-class window seat on a Delta Airlines flight when a soldier in his uniform came aboard. I asked if he wanted my seat.

"No thank you, sir, that is not necessary," he said. I insisted, and we swapped seats.

As I wandered to the coach section and took my new center seat between two chubby guys, I started to feel sorry for myself and focused on the negative. *I'm getting too old for this,* I thought. *I bend over to pull up my socks and think, What else can I accomplish while I'm way down here? I'm losing hair on the top of my head and growing it in places I don't even need it, with the only hope that the hair in my right ear will grow long enough that I can comb it up over the top of my head and fake everybody out. I go to bed healthy and wake up injured, and all I did was lie there.* Then it dawned on me: This soldier had been away from his family for an entire year, wearing eighty-five to one hundred pounds of combat gear in temperatures that reach 120 to 140 degrees Fahrenheit from May to August.

I looked up to find the guy I had been sitting next to in first class walking down the aisle. He told me I had made everybody feel guilty, and so he had given up his seat to the next soldier who boarded the plane. I found it amusing that this man's new seat was also in the center of the row between two chubbier guys. He was so stuck he couldn't even turn around to complain! Before we took off, two other men from first class had given up their seats to soldiers.

We landed, I checked in to my hotel, had a good night's sleep, arose the next morning, and entered the ballroom to make my speech. I was the keynote speaker for a national convention of five thousand people, and wouldn't you know it? The man who introduced me was the guy who had sat next to me in first class! Moral of the story? People are watching. As I have realized again and again, showing our respect and appreciation for the covenant service of our troops encourages others to celebrate it, too, and still others to undertake that and other kinds of covenant service. Little by little, the world becomes a better, more decent, more humane place.

(I have had many wonderful, fulfilling experiences while swapping seats with our troops. I challenge you to do the same. You will discover as I have that service transforms both the giver *and* the receiver.)

Operation Smile

In affirming and validating covenant service, we must also be sure to show our support for all those truly significant individuals in civilian life who feel called to help people around the world in desperate need. I have seen such people in action as a member of the International Board of Governors of Operation Smile, a humanitarian organization whose plastic surgeons and critical care pediatric nurses volunteer their time to perform cleft lip and palate surgeries on underprivileged, needy children. As of 2012, we have operated on more than 160,000 children in 60 developing countries, conducting over 100 missions per year.

The doctors and nurses of Operation Smile are so committed to service before self that they often travel into war-torn nations to deliver their medical miracles. Serving the wonderful and courageous Iraqi people is no exception. We had a plan to operate on 110 Iraqi children with severe facial deformities, including 29 under the age of two. But because of excessive security challenges and diplomatic red tape, it became impossible for our team to actually go into Baghdad. No worries. We simply organized a mission to transport the children with their parents, medical volunteers, and 9 Iraqi doctors (210 people total) across the desert in several buses on a twenty-four-hour ride to Amman, Jordan. Halfway there, terrorist insurgents boarded the buses, screaming, pointing guns and knives, and demanding that anyone belonging to the rival religious faction be identified and dragged off the buses for execution. No one responded. Miraculously, thirty minutes later the terrorists got off the buses without hurting anyone and disappeared into the night. The frightened Iraqi families and medical volunteers continued to Amman, and within days, the 110 surgeries had been successfully completed.

All 210 people on this mission felt terrified at the idea of making the long bus ride home. Even the bus drivers refused to go. I received a phone call from my dear friend Michael Nebeker, whose sister Susan was on this mission and had reported the details to him over the phone. Then Dr. Bill Magee, founder along with his wife, Kathy, of Operation Smile, called to see if I could use my relationship with the U.S. Air Force to help. I had just spoken at the World Command Chiefs Conference for my friend and hero Gerald Murray, command chief master sergeant of the Air Force, and so I phoned him right after hanging up with Dr. Magee. Knowing how important it is for the United States to win hearts and minds with "soft power," Murray said he could get this thing done if we generated a sponsor letter from a senator or congressman.

Senator John Warner (R–Virginia) and Congressman Trent Franks (D–Arizona), with the incredible support from my dear friend Senator Orrin Hatch (R–Utah), composed the letter and then hand-delivered it to Secretary of Defense Donald Rumsfeld. Chief Murray conferred with Air Force Chief of Staff General T. Michael Moseley and within twenty-four hours sent two C-17 transport jets from Baghdad to Amman to rescue these 210 people. When they landed safely at the Baghdad International Airport, the families and medical volunteers walked down the stairs with their now beautiful babies and brand-new smiles. They knelt down in thanksgiving to kiss the ground of their homeland, and then stood to cheer and thank the military men and women who had loved them and unselfishly served them that day.

The patients served by Operation Smile are frequently no less significant than the organization's staff or the members of America's armed forces. One man in the Philippines, twenty-three-year-old José, had a three-pound tumor growing from his chin that was so large and grotesque that his family kept him hidden from public view his entire life, thinking him possessed by the devil. No one would hire him to work, and he went outside only at night, hiding his tumor behind a bandana. When José heard that Operation Smile was coming to perform free surgeries, he left his village on a three-and-a-half-day journey to our hospital facility in Manila. It was literally "planes, trains, and automobiles" as he walked over a rugged mountain pass, forged a river, and trekked untold miles along dusty backroads until he finally arrived in the city. Among hundreds of mothers, fathers, and their small children sleeping on the ground outside the hospital waiting for the morning to come, he was the lone adult hoping for a miracle.

As the screening process got under way, and the criterion for care was established, José learned that he did not qualify for treatment because he did not have a cleft lip or palate condition, and because of the limited time and resources, the priority of the mission was pediatric care. Sadly, he walked the three and a half days back home to his village. Six months later, word spread that Operation Smile was returning to Manila. Resolved to give it another chance, José again made the three-and-a-half-day journey only to be turned away a second time for the same reasons. This time, however, the hundreds who were turned away were promised that Operation Smile would return with greater resources, additional doctors, and an extended stay.

For the next six months, José counted the days. On the verge of suicide, he decided to try his luck one last time. He returned to Manila on the appointed day, passed the screening tests, and was scheduled to receive his surgery the next morning. As José was given his number and directed to the processing area, he started thinking about all the ways his life would immediately change. Then he noticed a devastated, crying mother whose little girl would have been next in line for surgery except for the lack of resources. José felt intense empathy for the girl. He told himself that he was old, and he didn't want her to go through life the way he had. In an unbelievable act of generosity, he gave his number to the little girl. With tears in his eyes, not knowing if he would ever have this chance again, José turned and slowly trekked his way home.

Upon learning of José, Dr. McGee tracked him down in his village. With the help of some donors, he arranged for José to be flown to Norfolk, Virginia, where Dr. McGee and a team of extraordinarily skilled surgeons performed nine surgeries over the space of several weeks to remove the three-pound tumor.

I first met José when we shared the program as keynote speakers at an International Operation Smile Leadership Conference. I was deeply touched when the handsome, smiling, confident, articulate José finished his speech by singing a song he had written about Operation Smile. We all gazed up at a huge photograph of him in a white tuxedo, standing next to his gorgeous wife, holding their beautiful newborn baby. This is what Operation Smile is all about: changing the world one person, one smile, one family, one village, one country, at a time! Learn how to get involved in Operation Smile and discover how incredibly rewarding it feels to become significant through covenant service.

The Bottom Line

Successful people obey the preparatory principle of commitment. Significant individuals at all levels live the advanced, highest Law of Covenant, and they perform covenant service. The best way to find ourselves is to lose ourselves in the service of others. Service transforms the servant *and* the served. Whoever renders service to many puts himself in line for greatness—great wealth, great return, great satisfaction, great reputation, and great love. As Rabindranath Tagore said, "I slept and dreamt that life was joy. I awoke and saw that life was service. I acted and behold, service was joy."

Four Suggested Action Steps to Learning Covenant Service

1. Create a sign that reads WHAT DID YOU DO FOR SOMEONE ELSE TODAY? and showcase it in a visible place, such as on your refrigerator door or bathroom mirror.

2. Begin with the "low-hanging fruit": Look for little things you can do in your own home with your family—cleaning, cooking, lifting, pushing, doing dishes, tutoring, driving, listening. Do something more every day for a week.

3. Organize a reporting system (usually during Sunday dinner) allowing each family member to share what he or she did each day that week.

4. Expand the areas, venues, and circles of influence wherein you exercise service before self. Do something for someone else at work, in the neighborhood, at your children's school, at a children's cancer ward in a hospital; volunteer at a retirement home or rehabilitation center; join a service club such as Rotary, Kiwanis, Optimists, or Elks, and get involved on their local and national committees; go into the community and raise money for charitable organizations, such as Operation Smile, the Children's Miracle Network, the American Cancer Society, the American Diabetes Association, and especially the U.S. military's Wounded Warriors. I highly recommend that you embrace a charity of your choice and organize your company involvement into a culture of covenant service before self.

Forgive Instead of Apologize

The willingness to forgive is a sign of spiritual and emotional maturity. It is one of the great virtues to which we should all aspire. Imagine a world filled with individuals willing both to apologize and to accept an apology. Is there any problem that could not be solved among people who possessed the humility and largeness of spirit and soul to do either—or both—when needed?

—GORDON HINCKLEY

The eleven laws we've examined so far have given you a feeling for the journey that is significance, a sense of why it is so difficult yet worthwhile. I hope I've challenged your sacred cows, and you've experienced a shift in how you think about and relate to your everyday life. But how do you know you're *really* living these laws? Significance is ultimately about action, not merely thought. Often we think we're living significant lives, only to find that we falter embarrassingly in moments of conflict with others. When we're upset and we raise our voices, judge with prejudice, put others down, lose our calm, fail to listen, become irrational, or get moody and depressed, this is not caused by whatever is applying the pressure on us. This is latent anger peeking out, the legacy of past, unresolved conflicts.

Successful people can and do attempt to move beyond past conflicts by merely offering apologies—expressions of remorse—for their transgressions. While that's important (as we'll see), it doesn't go far enough to get at the root of the problem. There is a way to ensure that egotism and the fires of anger have truly been extinguished. Only when we go beyond merely proffering apologies and also *humble ourselves enough to unconditionally forgive those who have wronged us* (including ourselves) will we be humble, meek, and teachable enough to want to obey, persevere, stretch, trust, seek whole truth, win, do right, experience harmony, accept others, strive to be loved and needed, and establish a covenant to serve. True, deep forgiveness can be difficult to bestow, and many of us never even come close to managing it. Yet psychiatrists, psychologists, and psychotherapists all confirm that everyone in the world can and should forgive, and if significance is what you seek, you have no other choice.

Merely apologizing usually doesn't resolve our underlying anger, because most apologies are facile and have a formal quality to them; they don't reflect an underlying process of spiritual growth and self-reckoning. We've all heard empty professions of remorse from politicians and celebrities, sometimes given in the expectation that their partner in conflict will in turn give *them* an apology. Successful people have made education, internships, first job, and career all about themselves, and so they stay at a superficial level and have difficulty healing their hearts enough to make meaningful changes in behavior. Significant people, because of their intense and habitual focus on others, can transcend anger and hate on the deepest level, stretching past their egos in an almost miraculous act of personal purification, and changing their behavior forever in the process. Their hearts open and they extend forgiveness both to themselves and to others, without the expectation (in the case of conflict with others) of receiving forgiveness in turn.

The minute we unconditionally forgive is the moment we let go of every excuse we have ever had for failing, falling, and saying and doing the wrong thing. We let down our guard, lose our defense mechanisms, and remove the walls we once hid behind that kept the world from seeing our insecurities, faults, weaknesses, and limitations. The moment we unconditionally forgive is the moment when we actually admit we are not always right—the most difficult thing for a leader to do. Offering forgiveness means you have a tender heart; a real "macho man" is *velvet and steel*—compassionate enough to never fight the onslaught of laughter or tears because he is always authentic in every moment, yet strong enough to fight, protect, and defend everything and anyone who is good, clean, pure, positive, and right. Offering forgiveness is the ultimate expression of love and respect, and as you will discover in the next few pages, the law that enables us to keep our power and authority in check, ensuring that we treat all people as we ourselves want to be treated.

To become significant beings, we must do the hard, steady, inner work of forgiving others unconditionally—rather than simply stating "I apologize"—so that we can learn from the past and address what we will do in the future to behave better. In addressing unresolved conflict, we must be strong, look to our divine natures, and thereby free ourselves once and for all from anger's fiery hold. Although many of us sustain a certain amount of residual anger in our lives, there are no shortcuts here. We cannot live and obey the other eleven Laws of Significance without replacing the weaker, negative, reactive mind-sets of anger and hate (and the periodic expressions of remorse that accompany them) with the positive, proactive, highest law known as forgiving others.

The Scourge of Anger and Hate

Let me say a bit more about why resolving conflict and overcoming feelings of anger and hate is both possible and worth the supreme effort. Anger and hate may be natural and inevitable parts of life, yet we don't have to become angry, hateful people. Sustaining negative feelings—holding them in our hearts—is a learned behavior, much like sustaining love and acceptance. Anger is nothing more than masked fear. Whenever I have become angry at someone (or at myself) for doing something displeasing or breaking a rule, I have gotten dramatic because I feared this person would do the same wrong thing again, and I wanted to emphasize that this would be a bad idea. Conversely, when an angry person feels confident that we won't make the same mistake again, she is no longer afraid on the inside and therefore no longer appears angry on the outside.

Many of us try to dissociate anger from agency, telling ourselves that an emotion we cannot control has victimized us. We say that we "lost our temper," implying something accidental, involuntary. "He made me mad," we say, also implying a lack of control. Neither is correct, because nobody *makes* us angry. We *decide* to become angry, which means we can decide *not* to become angry.

"But I can't help myself," you may say.

"Get a grip," I say. "Choose your battles."

Throwing a tantrum and managing our reactions are strategies we learn in handling disappointment. We simply choose the one that has proven effective for us in the past. Have you ever noticed how seldom we lose control when frustrated by our boss, but how often we do when annoyed by strangers, friends, or family?

As a practical matter, using anger to get what we want is an elementary way of thinking, behaving, and managing. Anger is futile—like drinking poison and expecting the person we are angry with to die; it only begets more angry reactions from others. Hatred is even more destructive, leaving a crazed feeling and negative emotional aftermath that haunts us, drains us of our energy, and leads to the extinction of values. Projecting calm and deep disappointment expresses our hurt far more effectively, thus inspiring real behavior change. Only when we direct anger at ourselves can it become a force for good. Usually when we are sad, we don't do anything. But when we get angry at what we did and learn lessons from it, we bring about a change.

Letting It All Out

Prideful people, even those who may have achieved success, are often easily offended and slow to forgive. They enjoy keeping others in their debt in order to justify their injured feelings. Willingness to forgo vengeance does not undo a tragedy or pardon any wrong, but it does constitute a first step toward a more hopeful future. Spencer Kimball wrote, "To be in the right we must forgive, and we must do so without regard to whether or not our enemy is sincere in his transformation, or whether or not he asks our forgiveness." Marion Hanks explains, "Our true freedom, pure joy, and lasting satisfaction in this life depend upon our willingness and capacity to forgive wrongs committed against us. Even if it appears that another may be deserving of our resentment or hatred, none of us can afford to pay the price of resenting or hating because of what it does to us. May we rid ourselves of pettiness and foolish pride, and love and forgive, in order that we may be friends with ourselves and with others."

Those who find forgiveness hard in times of conflict typically are betraying themselves. In the Arbinger Institute's bestselling book *Leadership and Self-Deception*, the authors state: "An act contrary to what I feel I should do for another is called self-betrayal. When I betray myself I begin to see the world in a way that justifies my self-betrayal. When I see the world in a self-justifying way, my view of reality becomes distorted."

Harboring hatred and anger is similar to being constipated. Bloating and cramping causes continual misery, and no matter where you go or what you do, you cannot escape the pain. Releasing the poisonous toxins from your body is the only solution. The resulting feeling is total bliss, a restoration back to your old self. Likewise, forgiveness—whether of ourselves or of others—brings with it an incredible change in our minds and hearts. Obtaining forgiveness is not a matter of deserving—it's a matter of believing. Carrying a grudge is like being stung to death by just one bee. On the positive side, refusal to retaliate is the beginning of personal purification from resentment and bitterness. It is the beginning of healing.

Real Healing

Let's deepen our understanding of forgiveness as healing. Healing in the physical body occurs in one of two ways. If the wound is superficial and the bleeding easily stopped, you stitch the outer layer of skin and affix a bandage, and the healing happens from the outside-in. But if the wound is deep with a jagged edge, such outside-in healing isn't enough: The surface may appear closed, but underneath it all and unbeknownst to us, the wound is festering and infection is setting in. Such wounds only heal if we keep them open long enough to heal from the inside out, one layer and one step at a time.

Deep emotional wounds that come from the loss of a loved one, a devastating divorce, shattered dreams, being downsized at work, or any kind of significant conflict with others require inside-out healing. So do wounds from conflicts we have not rectified within ourselves. We need to keep our emotional wounds open not so that we give our antagonists time to say and feel what we want them to, *but so that we can achieve a meaningful stretch in our own attitudes and awareness.* Before we can forgive others and heal any wounds we sustain at their hands, we must first learn to forgive ourselves. Taking a long, hard, honest look in the mirror, we shift our focus away from others' misdeeds and instead acknowledge only our *own*, accepting ourselves with all of our flaws and foibles. We can't control how others treat us, and we sure can't make them forgive us or even accept our superficial apologies. All we can do is work on ourselves, take responsibility for our *own* role in the conflict, and resolve to move on. Forgiving others as I define it is an internally driven process, something we ultimately do *to* ourselves and *for* ourselves.

Intense self-reflection makes our egos vulnerable and is exqui-sitely painful, so most of us procrastinate until absolutely forced into forgiveness. That's unfortunate: Until we come to take the measure of ourselves and extend forgiveness, we can never accept others fully; we can merely tolerate them (see Law 9, "Accept Others Instead of Judging Them"). Our own unresolved feelings simmer within us, poisoning our experience in the present. To counteract our fear of confronting ourselves, we should remember the wonderful fruits of this hard work. The process of forgiving others (and ourselves) al-lows us to simultaneously feel forgiven by ourselves. Just as with physical injuries, healing also allows us to emerge stronger at the very place of the wound, eventually becoming complete to the point where we remember the hurt no more.

I regard the task of extending forgiveness as a five-step process. First, in shifting ourselves away from a victim's mentality in which we blame others, *we recognize that we blew it*, that our present situa-tion is unhappy, and we know that if we are to see any change, we must make it ourselves. At this stage, we finally get sick and tired of being sick and tired (some also call this "hitting rock bottom," where the only way is up). We admit our *own* wrongdoings, knowing that holding on to horrible habits or resentments hurts us more than any-one else by keeping us from living fully in the present, the only mo-ment in which we can live peacefully and positive and free of past negatives.

Second, in keeping our attention focused on ourselves, not the person we're forgiving, we feel *genuine and deep remorse* for any mis-deeds we ourselves may have committed. Some go astray at this step. Take President Bill Clinton: He admitted to and apologized for having sexual relations with Monica Lewinsky in the White House's sacred Oval Office. But, we must ask, was he just annoyed that he got caught, or did he feel genuine remorse for doing something wrong? Before we can progress in our quest to forgive others, we must admit to ourselves whether our remorse reflects embarrassment or flows from genuine sorrow.

Confession, the third step in the forgiveness process, represents the beginning of our personal purification, which is the bottom-line reason we forgive in the first place. Forgiving is not forgetting or condoning what others have done; rather, it is taking *100 percent* responsibility for what we have done. In confession, we perform a man-in-the-mirror, self-auditing inventory check in which we admit what we did and why we did what we did. No excuses, no reasons, only an acknowledgment that we did what we did. Yes, confession is difficult and embarrassing, but once we have achieved that level of honesty with ourselves, it is easier to confess to those we have offended, admitting that we broke a law, violated their trust, broke their heart, or ruined their reputation, again with no expectation of a similar *confession* from them.

This brings us to the apology part of *confession*. Yes, expressing remorse *does* play a role in the forgiveness process. But unlike all the usual rote apologies, this is a real, meaningful one grounded in self-reflection and an honest intent to transcend past patterns of behaviors. Expressing humility and strength and the delivery of an unsolicited, heartfelt apology with no strings attached marks the point in the process where we empower ourselves to forgive ourselves, and consequently, our partners in conflict. Those who can admit that they have made a mistake really are, as Mahatma Gandhi said, the strongest among us.

Our personal audits remind us that we can always get better, do better, be better. This leads us to commit to the fourth step of the forgiveness process: *restitution.* No, we don't forgive others because they have paid *us* restitution. We forgive them in the process of making amends ourselves for our part in the conflict. If we have stolen something, we return it—never mind what our antagonist did. If we have destroyed someone's confidence in us, we do everything in our power to restore that trust by once again being predictable over a period of time—never mind if our antagonist is behaving spitefully. Restitution is more than *being* sorry; it's *doing* sorry. It's forever forsaking our negative thoughts, feelings, and offensive behavior, and committing never to do it again, irrespective of such a commitment from our partner in conflict. And no, it is not a long and arduous task.

Remembering it no more is the fifth and final step of the forgiveness process. Because we have purified ourselves in our own minds, we free ourselves to surpass anger, move forward, and let the mistakes, failures, and trespasses we have suffered drift away. Regardless of whether the other person responds or changes, part of this final step is to keep willing love and goodness to them so our relationship will continue to move ahead. No more blaming the community or another person and making them the scapegoat for your having fallen out of favor. No more holding grudges. And as strange as it sounds, no more holding grudges against yourself.

In Sophocles' *Oedipus Rex*, Oedipus does some terrible things, and when he finally faces his conscience, he feels that the only way he can make amends is to accept punishment. But because no one will apply the punishment, he decides to be his own judge and jury, and to punish himself. Consequently, he blinds himself. What a waste! Forgiving ourselves is the prerequisite to forgiving others, which in turn is the catalyst for internal healing and the solving of every relationship challenge, in every generation, personally and professionally. Forgiveness's extraordinary, long-lasting, far-reaching impact on individuals and society at large is sometimes unbelievable, often reverently beautiful, and always inspirational, and it all begins with *us*.

Forgiveness in the Skies

When forgiveness happens, even if only for a moment, it can bring about positive and unforeseen long-term ramifications. One evening during my speaking tour to the combat troops in Iraq, I was dining with my escort General Al Peck and the base commander Colonel Blair Hansen in the mess tent in Baghdad. An officer interrupted our dinner with a message that the leadership of the new Iraqi Air Force wanted to join us. Three Iraqi officers were shown to our table, and we embarked on a friendly discussion of the aircraft each of us flew. The Iraqi colonel flew a French-made Mirage, and the Iraqi major and captain each flew Russian MIGs. When General Peck and Colonel Hansen explained that they had been F-15 drivers, the two Iraqi MIG pilots grew excited and exclaimed that the F-15 was the world's most beautiful and best-engineered fighter jet. In fact, they explained that one day while on a mission they saw two F-15s and wanted so badly to get a closer look that they crossed into forbidden airspace in pursuit.

The restricted airspace was called Operation Northern Watch, which was a U.S. European Command Combined Task Force (CTF) charged with protecting the Kurdish people from being massacred by the Iraqi military. This required the Coalition forces to enforce its own no-fly zone above the 36th Parallel in Iraq. Its mission began on January 1, 1997. For the first year of the mission, northern Iraq was quiet, with no combat between Coalition aircraft and Iraqi forces. However, in December 1998, Iraq announced they would no longer recognize the no-fly zones and urged their troops and pilots to attack Coalition aircraft. From December 1998 to March 1999, U.S. aircraft over northern Iraq came under almost daily fire from Iraqi surface-to-air missile sites and anti-aircraft guns. U.S. aircraft responded by bombing Iraqi air-defense sites, which fired on them. Despite Saddam Hussein offering a $14,000 reward for downing a Coalition aircraft, no warplanes were shot down.

The Iraqi pilots continued to tell their story, explaining that before they could turn back, one of them had his cockpit warning start flashing and beeping, indicating he had been locked on by one of the F-15s, and that a heat-seeking air-to-air missile would be coming his way soon. He told us he prayed, thought of his wife and children, and braced himself to die. However, for some reason the F-15 pilot did not fire his missile, and the Iraqi pilots flew safely home.

General Peck asked the Iraqis when this experience occurred. They told him the exact day and time, and he smiled. "Colonel Hansen, do you remember what happened to you and me on that day?"

Colonel Hansen looked at the Iraqi pilots and replied, "Yes. We were the two F-15 pilots. After locking on, General Peck radioed that he didn't think you guys were causing any harm and asked me if I thought we should forgive your navigation mistake and let you off the hook. I agreed and we let you go."

The Iraqi pilots jumped to their feet and joyfully toasted Hanson and Peck for saving their lives—for allowing them to live! With hugs and handshakes, they showed us photos of their families as we agreed how great it was that, despite being brutal enemies only a few years before, we now were forgiving friends and brothers-in-arms committed to building a better, free, and prosperous Iraq.

I purposefully chose war as the backdrop for concluding this discussion on forgiveness that we may once and for all acknowledge the long-term negative ramifications and generational consequences that will occur if we don't forgive. Are there any moments in the course of a day when you have the opportunity to exercise forgiveness? If so, please take them. Even these seemingly forgettable, incidental gestures can make a difference beyond your wildest imagination.

The Bottom Line

Successful people merely offer apologies, remaining ensnared in a weaker, negative mind-set of anger and hate. Individuals who live lives of significance choose to obey and experience the advanced, highest Law of Forgiveness. As leaders, managers, coaches, educators, and parents, we must teach that good character entails not only doing the right thing simply because it's the right thing to do, but also doing the right thing in the aftermath of someone having done the wrong thing. While obedience is the first and foremost universal law upon which all success and significance is predicated, forgiveness is the deepest law and the most intimate two-way connection in the universe. Every time we look into someone's eyes and sincerely say, "I'm sorry, I unconditionally love you and need you, I forgive you, and thank you for forgiving me," we move humanity closer to that time where the lion will lie with the lamb, because there is peace on earth and goodwill toward all.

Four Suggested Action Steps for Learning to Forgive Unconditionally

1. At the first approach of anger, remind yourself that you, too, have voiced your insensitive opinion in an emotionally fueled conversation, disappointed a loved one, angered an associate, or made a hard choice that left someone brokenhearted. Remember that you, too, have needed someone to give you a break in order for you to continue, and that what goes around comes around. The quickest way to get back at those who harm us physically or emotionally is to forgive them and to shower them with service, positive energy, and fellowship!

2. At work, remember that humans naturally tend to exercise unrighteous dominion the minute they gain a little bit of power. But no power, influence, or judgment can be or ought to be maintained except by persuasion, gentleness, meekness, and kindness. If you reprimand another sharply, afterward show that person a display of unconditional forgiveness.

3. Avoid prejudging by realizing that similarity creates comfort, while difference creates rewards and importance. If two people agree on everything, it means one of them is not necessary.

4. Make a list of individuals who have offended you. Go back as many years as necessary. Research where they live today. Swallow your pride, and if financially and logistically possible, make arrangements to go and visit them. An e-mail or a text or a letter is unacceptable. It must be a face-to-face meeting, arranged in a quiet place where you can talk and cry and do whatever is required to bury the hatchet and forgive them. Begin by visiting with your individual family members first, then friends, neighbors, and coworkers, and then your enemies. Guaranteed, you will feel more loved, more needed, and more peaceful than you have ever felt in your entire life, which will turn your previous successes into lasting significance.

Epilogue

A Significant Life

Ye live not for yourselves; ye cannot live for yourselves; a thousand fibres connect you with your fellow-men, and along those fibres, as along sympathetic threads, run your actions as causes, and return to you as effects.

—HERMAN MELVILLE

I cannot end a book about how to live a life of significance without introducing you to a rose among thorns. I met her in chemistry class on the first day of my senior year in college. The professor challenged us to introduce ourselves to someone we did not know. Before I could move, a gentle hand touched my shoulder. I turned to find a wrinkled, older lady whose smile lit up her face like a Las Vegas street sign. "Hey, handsome, my name is Rose. I am eighty-seven years old. Do you want to get lucky?"

I laughed and replied, "You incredible, gorgeous babe, I'm all yours!" We hugged, and the rest is history.

"Why are you in college at your young, innocent age?" I asked.

"I'm here looking for a rich husband," she joked. "You know, get married, have a couple of children, retire, travel." Laughing hysterically, I begged her to be serious. Her answer was simple but profound. "I always dreamed of having a college degree, and so I'm getting one. It is unfinished business. I refuse to die at the base of the mountain with my music stuck inside me. I want to die while climbing."

We became friends, and over the course of the school year, Rose became a campus icon, generating attention everywhere she went. In the third week of school, she even got a tattoo. I teased her that I was hurt it didn't say "Dan the Man." Of course, it was a magnificent little red rose.

Once a day, as Rose walked between classes, she would stop at the library plaza to rest her weary legs. With the huge fountain spraying and the breeze blowing mist into the air, Rose would hold court. Within minutes, up to two hundred students sat at her feet basking in her attitude of gratitude and ode to joy. They say wisdom is the gift of the elderly, and Rose epitomized the quip, "When an old woman dies, an entire library burns to the ground."

Every person who interacted with Rose left her saying, "I like me best when I'm with you; I want to see you again." In fact, Rose was so inspirational that we had her speak at an end-of-year football banquet. I'll never forget the laugh she provided when she stepped to the podium and accidentally dropped her speech. With 3x5 cards all over the floor, Rose calmly leaned into the microphone and said, "I'm sorry I'm so nervous. I gave up beer for Lent and this whiskey is killing me!" I still have my notes from that evening all those years ago and have reconstructed Rose's remarks to the best of my ability. I know I and the audience will never forget her wisdom.

First, dream. You've got to have a dream. If you don't have a dream, how are you going to make a dream come true? When you lose your dreams, you die. That's why we have so many people walking the halls of life who are dead and don't even know it. As I've walked around campus this year, I've noticed how many of you college guys are still wearing your old high school letterman jackets. I wanted to tap each one of you on the head and say, "Yo, buddy. I know you used to be a stud-muffin-hunk-of-burnin'-love, but when your horse dies, dismount. Stop living in the past. Get a life. Dream a new dream. Get a new horse!"

Second, act. We are all, it seems, saving ourselves for the senior prom and forgetting that somewhere along the way we must learn to dance. No one is going to compel you to work, for the simple reason that a man who requires to be driven is not worth the driving.

Third, grow up. There is a giant difference between growing older and growing up. If you are nineteen years old and lie in bed for one full year and don't do one productive thing, you will turn twenty years old. If I am eighty-seven years old and stay in bed for a year and don't do anything and don't get any better or smarter, I will turn eighty-eight. Whoop-de-do! Anybody can grow older. That doesn't take any talent or ability. May we all continue to grow up by keeping at least one major dream alive. Remember, we're as young as we feel but seldom as important!

Fourth, leave no regrets. The only people who fear death are those with regrets. My friend Marjorie Hinckley pretty much summed up what it means to be fully alive when she told me she didn't want to drive up to the pearly gates in a shiny sports car, wearing beautifully tailored clothes, with long, perfectly manicured fingernails and her hair expertly coifed. She wanted to drive up in an old station wagon that has mud on the wheels from taking kids to Boy Scout camp; to be there with a smudge of peanut butter on her shirt from making sandwiches for a sick neighbor's children; to be there with a little dirt under her fingernails from helping to weed someone's garden; to be there with children's sticky kisses on her cheeks and the tears of a friend on her shoulder. She wants the creator to know she was really here and that she really lived. Too many love things and use people. We must love people and use things. All of the greatest accomplishments, successes, and possessions mean nothing if you are alone and only making a living instead of a difference.

Rose concluded her short and memorable speech and then waited at the door to shake each of our hands and give us a copy of the following quote by James Talmage:

Promise yourself today to be so strong that nothing can disturb your peace of mind;

To look on the bright side of everything and make your dreams
  come true;
To think the best, to forget the mistakes of the past, and to press on
  to better things;
To give so much time to improving yourself that you don't have time
  to criticize others;
To be too large for worries, too noble for anger, too large for fear,
And too happy to permit the presence of trouble;
To think well of yourself and to proclaim this force to the world
Not in loud words but in great works.

At semester's end, Rose walked across the stage to receive her university diploma to a long, thunderous, standing ovation. Unbeknownst to anyone, she had been battling cancer, and two weeks after graduation, believing in her heart that she had run life's race, won the fight, reached the highest measure of her full potential, and left everybody she encountered in better shape than she had found us, Rose died peacefully in her sleep.

Four days later, more than two thousand college students attended her funeral to pay tribute to this amazing human being who taught by example that it's never too late to become more of who we already are. No one mourned her death. Rather, we celebrated the passionate life Rose led. We didn't cry because it was over. We smiled because it happened! Rose never did anything famous and never made a lot of money. She did leave her family, friends, and college better than when she found us. Rose was in a class all by herself—okay, maybe not by herself, but whatever class she's in as a whole, it doesn't take too long to call the roll!

To understand death, we must appreciate the purpose of life, which is to become significant. One big, cosmic meaning does not exist for all of us. We have only the meaning we each give to our lives—an individual meaning, an individual plot, like an individual novel, a book for each person. The least of things with a meaning is worth more in life than the greatest of things without it. And since we all die, set apart only by the details of our lives and actions, I urge you to fight your fears and take the risks necessary to be who you truly are. May you now and forever more obey, persevere, stretch, trust, seek whole truth, win, do right, experience harmony, accept, love and be needed, forge a covenant to serve, and forgive.

I began this book by contrasting success with significance. I'll end with one final distinction that has been implicit along the way. Achieving success is a pursuit of finite triviality usually measured by income, whereas the pursuit of significance is endless, creative, even artful (hence, the title of this book) and always measured by the outcomes it brings for those around us. As I've traveled the world and interviewed presidents, sheikhs, and the super-rich, I've discovered that many of their lives have not been as easy or as pleasurable as many would assume. These merely successful people have given themselves over to fortune and fame, surrendering, in turn, their capacity to live as well-adjusted, fulfilled human beings. Yes, I admire the way these individuals have excelled, but I've seen up close the costs of a single-minded focus on success.

You are one person among seven billion on this earth. Yes, you are unique and special; there are no duplicate fingerprints for any two people who have ever lived. But the path to significance occurs against the prior and obvious background of our own *insignificance*. Given how small we all are, it is only through our hard work and actions that we can take on meaning in the minds of others. Significance is the legacy we leave behind because of the good we've done, not only after we die (the old will, the young may), but especially while we live. Being significant must be startling, unexpected—just as Rose was startling and unexpected to me. It must come to a world that is not prepared for it. I agree with the insight of Oliver Wendell Holmes, "As for the excellent little wretches who grow up in what they are taught, with never a scruple or a query . . . they signify nothing in the intellectual life of the race."

So, what will it be for you? Will you be remembered for having made the world a better place? In times of crisis or difficulty, I rediscover my own answers to these questions by counting my blessings in life and giving thanks to my family, friends, coworkers, and teammates. I come away motivated to once again hunker down and live by the Twelve Highest Universal Laws of Life-Changing Leadership.

I challenge you to do the same.

THE END—WHICH IS THE BEGINNING!
TO CONTINUE . . . GO BACK TO PAGE 1!

Acknowledgments

To my beloved Kelly, Danny, Natalie, Nikola, McCall, and Alexandrea;

To Paul Clark, Bill Gibbs, Tom Thorum, Mrs. Smart, and coaches Grant Martin, Ted Weight, Dale Simon, Chuck Banker, Vince Zimmer, and Tom Gadd—for believing in me when no one else did;

To coach Jan Smith, Doug Miller, Lila Bjorklund, Dr. Normand Gibbons, Russ Anderson, Craig Zwick, Don Pugh, Warren Pugh, Fred Ball, and Jerry Howells—for giving me my start in the speaking business;

To Zig Ziglar, Dr. Jim and Karen Koeninger, Stephen Cosgrove, Mickey Fisher, Jennifer Lapine, Pat Mutch, Mark Victor Hansen, and Jack Canfield—for tutoring me on how to become successful;

To S. Wayne, Ruby, Sam and Debbie Clark, Doc and Barb Sansom, Dr. Hal Bourne, Bob Raybould, Bill Kimball, Royden and Ali Derrick, Robert and Catherine Pedersen, Philip Gibson, Mark Tuttle, Mont Beardall, Gary Mangum, Mark Monsen, Blain Hope, Todd Peterson, Colin and Teresa Dunn, Robert Pederson, Todd Morgan, Brent Bowen,

Scott Buie, Walter Plumb, Scott Forsythe, Ron Ferrin, Jason Boren, David Ayre, David Spafford, Todd Cook, L. Todd Larsen, Dave Terry, Dennis Webb, Joe Lake, Rick Larsen, Dr. Bill and Kathy Magee and Stephen Munn—for mentoring me on why and how to be significant;

To U.S. Air Force General Hal Hornburg (ret.) and U.S. Air Force Major General Johnny Weida (ret.)—for teaching me the significance of unselfish sacrifice, unwavering integrity, commitment to service before self, and relentlessly seeking excellence in all I do;

And to Nena Madonia—my friend and amazing literary agent at Dupree/Miller—for believing in everything about me; to Simon Sinek—a bestselling author and extraordinary speaker—for believing in the power of networking and recommending my philosophy to the publishing world; to Adrian Zackheim—publisher and literary icon at Portfolio / Penguin—for believing in the power of my work and making me one of his authors; to Jillian Gray and Bria Sandford—my extraordinary associate editors and project managers at Portfolio / Penguin—for believing in the timeliness of my message; to Daniel Hope—my incredible first iteration editor; to Seth Schulman—my magnificent manuscript editor who finely tuned my thoughts and smoothed out my delivery; to Jeevan Sivasubramaniam—executive managing editor of Berrett-Kohler—who out of the goodness of his heart encouraged me and helped me to focus my thoughts into what has become this book; to my friend John Ingram—chairman of Ingram Book Group—for guiding and supporting me in every way possible; and to Laura Calchera—who has been the heart and soul of my business for over a decade. I love all of you and take great pride in calling each of you my friend!

Appendix

The Twelve Laws of Significance

Law 1: Practice Obedience Instead of Free Will Agency

Law 2: Exercise Perseverance Instead of Patience

Law 3: Proactively Stretch Instead of Change

Law 4: Trust Predictability Instead of Hope and Faith

Law 5: Know the Whole Truth Instead of Believing What You Think

Law 6: Focus on Winning Instead of Team

Law 7: Do Right Instead of Seeking to Be Best

Law 8: Experience Harmony Instead of Forcing Balance

Law 9: Accept Others Instead of Judging Them

Law 10: Love and Be Needed Instead of Romanced and Used

Law 11: Establish Covenants Instead of Making Commitments

Law 12: Forgive Instead of Apologize

Index

About the Author

Dan Clark is the CEO of Clark Success Systems, an international high-performance consulting firm; a university professor; an award-winning athlete who fought his way back from a paralyzing injury that cut short his football career; a bestselling author; an adventurer; a philanthropist; a Gold Record songwriter/recording artist; and one of the most sought-after speakers on the platform today.

In 2005, Clark was inducted into the National Speakers Hall of Fame, and Achievers North America and Achievers Europe have named Clark one of the Top Ten Speakers in the World.

In 1982, Clark was named an Outstanding Young Man of America and was sponsored into the National Speakers Association by world-renowned motivational teacher Zig Ziglar. Since then, Clark has spoken to more than 4 million people in more than 4,500 audiences, in 52 countries, on 6 continents, and to groups as diverse as Fortune 500 companies, NASA, Super Bowl Champions, Million Dollar Round Table, U.S. Department of Labor, the United Arab Emirates Festival of Thinkers, the United Nations World Congress, and to our combat troops in Iraq, Afghanistan, and Africa.

Clark is the author of twenty of his own books, including *Puppies for Sale,* which was made into a film at Paramount Studios starring Jack Lemmon. As a master storyteller, Clark has been published in more than forty million books and in forty languages worldwide and has appeared on more than five hundred television and radio programs, including *Oprah* and *Glenn Beck,* and was the cover story in *Millionaire Magazine.*

Clark's inspiring life has included soaring to the edge of space in a U-2 spy plane; flying fighter jets with the Air Force Thunderbirds; racing automobiles at Nurburgring; carrying the Olympic torch in the 2002 Winter Games; serving on the international board of governors of Operation Smile; serving with the Chief of Staff of the United States Air Force on his National Civic Leaders Board; and coaching high school football (winning the State 5A Championship in 2005). Most significant, Clark was honored as the 2012 Utah Father of the Year.

His Web site is www.danclarkspeak.com.